LawExpress
CONSUMER AND COMMERCIAL LAW

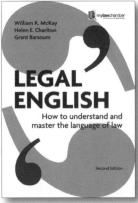

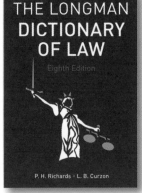

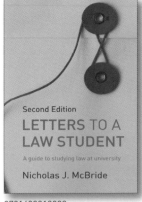

CONSUMER AND COMMERCIAL LAW

2nd edition

Judith Tillson, Barrister
Senior Lecturer in Law
Staffordshire University Law School

PEARSON

Harlow, England • London • New York • Boston • San Francisco • Toronto • Sydney • Auckland • Singapore • Hong Kong
Tokyo • Seoul • Taipei • New Delhi • Cape Town • São Paulo • Mexico City • Madrid • Amsterdam • Munich • Paris • Milan

Pearson Education Limited
Edinburgh Gate
Harlow
Essex CM20 2JE
England

and Associated Companies throughout the world

Visit us on the World Wide Web at:
www.pearson.com/uk

First published 2011
Second Edition published 2013

ISBN 978-1-4479-0076-4

British Library Cataloguing-in-Publication Data
A catalogue record for this book is available from the British Library

Library of Congress Cataloging-in-Publication Data
A catalog record for this book is available from the Library of Congress

10 9 8 7 6 5 4 3 2 1
16 15 14 13 12

Typeset in 10/12pt Helvetica Condensed by 3
Printed and bound in Malaysia (CTP-VP)

Contents

Supporting resources

Visit the *Law Express* series companion website at **www.pearsoned.co.uk/lawexpress** to find valuable student learning material including:

- A study plan test to help you assess how well you know the subject before you begin your revision
- Interactive quizzes to test your knowledge of the main points from each chapter
- Sample examination questions and guidelines for answering them
- Interactive flashcards to help you revise key terms, cases and statutes
- Printable versions of the topic maps and checklists from the book
- 'You be the marker' allows you to see exam questions and answers from the perspective of the examiner and includes notes on how an answer might be marked
- Podcasts provide point-by-point instruction on how to answer a typical exam question

Also: The companion website provides the following features:

- Search tool to help locate specific items of content
- E-mail results and profile tools to send results of quizzes to instructors
- Online help and support to assist with website usage and troubleshooting

For more information please contact your local Pearson Education sales representative or visit **www.pearsoned.co.uk/lawexpress**

Acknowledgements

Our thanks go to all reviewers who contributed to the development of this text, including students who participated in research and focus groups which helped to shape the series format.

Introduction

Many students study consumer and commercial law as discrete modules. Some students may study one rather than the other. However, this book treats them as complementary topics by examining areas common to both. Consumer and commercial law covers a wide range of subjects so module content will vary between institutions, but several topics will be common features, including sale of goods, agency law, credit, product liability, product safety and unfair trading practices. Because of the increasing influence of online contracts and distance selling, you are likely to be expected to appreciate the legal challenges presented by this mode of contracting. No doubt individual lecturers will emphasise particular topics in this diverse area. You should always refer to your lecturer or tutor and your course materials with any questions on what you will be expected to cover.

Another factor to bear in mind in preparing for the exam is that, inevitably, several topics will overlap and cannot be revised as discrete units. It is important to appreciate that studying consumer and commercial law will require that you have a sound basis in contract law, especially misrepresentation, unfair contract terms and remedies for breach.

The subject lends itself to problem questions which provide an opportunity for the examiner to assess your understanding of how different aspects of consumer and commercial law interlink. Don't be surprised to find that a problem on a topic such as product liability may also encompass aspects of sale of goods, negligence and privity. Likewise, questions calling for an analysis of unfair contract terms will expect you to be able to demonstrate detailed knowledge of aspects of sale of goods, misrepresentation and the supply of services. You will be expected to show clear understanding of the degree of statutory protection offered to those dealing on a commercial as well as consumer basis. When dealing with such multi-faceted problem questions, it is easy to digress into areas that are not relevant; it is also difficult to gauge which areas require a greater level of detailed analysis. Some questions may help you in this respect by allocating marks to different sections. The most difficult problems are those that include a range of issues within one detailed scenario. Always devise an outline plan to ensure that you deal with all relevant issues in a systematic and structured manner. It is a good idea to identify an issue, explain it and then apply it to the facts given.

With essay questions you should ensure that you understand what the question requires before outlining your plan. Essay questions tend to expose those who have a superficial understanding of a topic, as they call for detailed explanation of legal principles with application of case law and statute as well as critical comment. You will be expected to be able to highlight areas for criticism and potential reforms. You may be required to address a specific reform and carry out an evaluation, using recent authority, as to whether or not it is effective. A likely example would be the recent reform of the area of unfair trading practices. Keep to the issue by referring to the question and submitting suitable comment (based on your evaluation) where appropriate. Whether you are analysing a problem or writing an essay, make sure that you submit a conclusion.

This book is designed as a revision guide, not as a substitute for a textbook or your course notes. In order to promote quick understanding and effective revision, it gives you a clear overview of key topics in consumer and commercial law. It also provides a guide to suitable resources to develop a critical approach to examinations and assignments. The book focuses on common areas of misunderstanding and confusion, such as concepts of consumer status, the different heads of liability in product liability and the difference between sale by description and misrepresentation. In order to help you develop a confident attitude towards examinations, guidance is given in each chapter with regard to revision and exam tips, pointing out difficult areas and suggesting good approaches to a range of sample questions.

Finally, it is important that you are aware that the European Union intends to modernise and harmonise consumer and contract law by introducing a Directive on Consumer Rights. The proposed Directive will merge four existing EU Consumer Directives, namely: Sale of Consumer Goods and Guarantees (99/44/EC), Unfair Contract Terms (93/13/EC), Distance Selling (97/7/EC) and Doorstep Selling (85/577/EC). By means of a process of codification, the law in these areas will be updated to reflect technological changes in commerce and to try to overcome common problems with distance selling.

📖 **REVISION NOTE**

- Use this book to cement your knowledge of key issues in consumer and commercial law

- Be aware that there will be overlap between areas of consumer and commercial law – these topics cannot be studied as discrete entities

- Remember that this guide is intended as an aid to understanding and revision. You should use your course materials, textbooks and other resources to extend your knowledge

- Concentrate your revision on preparing to answer exam questions – particularly how you will construct your answers in an exam

Before you begin, you can use the study plan available on the companion website to assess how well you know the material in this book and identify the areas where you may want to focus your revision.

Guided tour

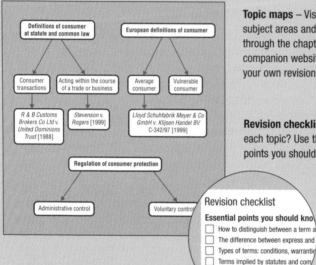

Topic maps – Visual guides highlight key subject areas and facilitate easy navigation through the chapter. Download them from the companion website to pin on your wall or add to your own revision notes.

Revision checklist – How well do you know each topic? Use these to identify essential points you should know for your exams. But don't panic if you don't know them all – the chapters will help you revise each point to ensure you are fully prepared. Print the checklists off the companion website and track your revision progress!

Revision checklist

Essential points you should know

- [ ] How to distinguish between a term a
- [ ] The difference between express and
- [ ] Types of terms: conditions, warrantie
- [ ] Terms implied by statutes and com
- [ ] Unfair contract terms relating to

Sample questions with Answer guidelines – Practice makes perfect! Read the question at the start of each chapter and consider how you would answer it. Guidance on structuring strong answers is provided at the end of the chapter. Try out additional sample questions online.

■ Sample question

Could you answer this question? Below is a typical problem question that could arise on this topic. Guidelines on answering the question are included at the end of this chapter, whilst a sample essay question and guidance on tackling it can be found on the companion website.

Assessment advice – Not sure how best to tackle a problem or essay question? Wondering what you may be asked? Use the assessment advice to identify the ways in which a subject may be examined and how to apply your knowledge effectively.

ASSESSMENT ADVICE

Essay questions

The question may take the form of a quotation upon which you are invited to comment. It is important to show, therefore, an understanding of the rationale behind consumer protection and why a party might prefer to achieve consumer status in a transaction. When describing various statutory definitions of consumer status, always highlight the potential loopholes in a definition by comparing and contrasting it with any other apt definition. Always use case law to illustrate how the courts utilise the definitions to reflect context, and take the opportunity to comment upon any discrepancies that may

Key definitions – Make sure you understand essential legal terms. Use the flashcards online to test your recall!

KEY DEFINITION: Expectation loss

Damages that aim to fulfil a contract by placing a party in the position they would have been in were the contract carried out, which may include loss of expected profits.

Key case and key statute – Identify and review the important elements of the essential cases and statutes you will need to know for your exams.

KEY CASE

Hong Kong Fir Shipping Co Ltd v. *Kawasaki Kisen Kaisha Ltd* [1962] 2 QB 26 (CA)
Concerning: innominate terms

Facts

~~ship~~ was chartered for two years by Kawasaki (the charterers) but was out of service ~~~~ weeks as it was declared 'unseaworthy'. The charterers mitigated their loss by ~~~~ssioning a cheaper charter elsewhere. When the ship was declared seaworthy, ~~~~terers repudiated the contract. The owners then sued for wrongful repudiation.

~~Pri~~nciple

~~~~erers were in breach. 'Seaworthiness' was not in this case a condition, but an ~~~~te term. It was neither a condition nor a warranty but the consequences of the ~~~~ were not serious enough to justify repudiation.

KEY STATUTE

Sale of Goods Act 1979, s. 37

When a seller, who is ready and willing ~~to~~ delivery within a reasonable time, the ~~buyer~~ after and keeping the goods while a~~waiting~~

~~~~arly any damages claimed by ~~~~than for loss of a bar~~~~

Make your answer stand out – This feature illustrates sources of further thinking and debate where you can maximise your marks. Use them to really impress your examiners!

✓ Make your answer stand out

Focus on the facts given in the problem in order to apply relevant sections of SGA 1979. Also, you need to identify Eve as a commercial rather than a consumer buyer. With regard to late delivery, you should mention that in the absence of contrary agreement, s. 29(3) SGA 1979 states that delivery should be within a reasonable time and what is reasonable depends on the circumstances. When addressing the delivery of incorrect quantities of plants you will need to detail Eve's

Exam tips – Feeling the pressure? These boxes indicate how you can improve your exam performance when it really counts.

EXAM TIP

Look out for problem questions in which there is a series of distance communications in contract negotiations, but where the contract is made face-to-face. This will not qualify as 'distance selling', neither will a one-off telephone or online order made by a customer. Also, it is important to understand that the term 'organised sales or service scheme' refers to a bespoke scheme for distance selling, such as an established home delivery service, rather than a one-off event.

Revision notes – Get guidance for effective revision. These boxes highlight related points and areas of overlap in the subject, or areas where your course might adopt a particular approach that you should check with your course tutor.

REVISION NOTE

With regard to damages you are advised to refer to the principles of expectation and reliance loss (see Chapter 2) as well as to the rules on remoteness of damage in *Hadley* v. *Baxendale* (see Chapter 5).

Glossary – Forgotten the meaning of a word? This quick reference covers key definitions and other useful terms.

Glossary of terms

The glossary is divided into two parts: key definitions and other useful terms. The key definitions can be found within the chapter in which they occur, as well as in the glossary below. These definitions are the essential terms that you must know and understand in order to prepare for an exam. The additional list of terms provides further definitions of useful terms and phrases which will also help you answer examination and coursework questions effectively. These terms are highlighted in the text as they occur but the definition can only be found here.

Don't be tempted to… – This feature underlines areas where students most often trip up in exams. Use them to spot common pitfalls and avoid losing marks.

! Don't be tempted to…

Take care not to underestimate the importance of the 2008 Regulations. These regulations on unfair trading have replaced the Trade Descriptions Act 1968 and cover *criminal*, rather than *civil*, liability.

Read to impress – Focus on these carefully selected sources to extend your knowledge, deepen your understanding, and earn better marks in coursework as well as in exams.

READ TO IMPRESS

De lacey, J. (1979) Selling in the Course of a Business under SGA, 62 *Modern Law Review*, Sept

Dobson, P. (2004) Exclusion Clause: Dealing as a Consumer, *Student Law Review* 43

MacDonald, E. (1995) In the Course of a Business – a Fresh Examination, 3 *Web Journal of Current Legal Issues*

Guided tour of the companion website

Book resources are available to download. Print your own **topic maps** and **revision checklists**!

Use the **study plan** prior to your revision to help you assess how well you know the subject and determine which areas need most attention. Choose to take the full assessment or focus on targeted study units.

'Test your knowledge' of individual areas with quizzes tailored specifically to each chapter. **Sample problem and essay questions** are also available with guidance on crafting a good answer.

Flashcards help improve recall of important legal terms and key cases and statutes. Available in both electronic and printable formats.

'You be the marker' gives you the chance to evaluate sample exam answers for different question types and understand how and why an examiner awards marks.

Download the **podcast** and listen as your own personal Law Express tutor guides you through a 10-15 minute audio session. You will be presented with a typical but challenging question and provided with a step-by-step explanation on how to approach the question, what essential elements your answer will need for a pass, how to structure a good response, and what to do to make your answer stand out so that you can earn extra marks.

All of this and more can be found when you visit **www.pearsoned.co.uk/lawexpress**

Table of cases and statutes

■ Cases

A v. National Blood Authority [2001] 3 All ER 298 **112, 122, 214**

Abouzaid v. Mothercare (UK) Ltd [2000] EWCA Civ 348 **112, 121, 214**

Aluminium Industrie Vaassen BV v. Romalpa Aluminium [1976] 1 WLR 676 **64, 70, 212**

Arcos Ltd v. E. A. Ronaasen & Son [1933] AC 470 **38, 48, 50, 210**

Armstrong v. Jackson [1917] 2 KB 822 **164, 177, 216**

Ashington Piggeries Ltd v. Christopher Hill Ltd [1971] 1 All ER 847 **38, 59, 210**

Attorney General of Belize v. Belize Telecom Ltd [2009] UKPC 11; [2009] 1 WLR 1988 **16, 23, 209**

Bannerman v. White (1861) 10 CBNS 844 **16, 19, 209**

Barry v. Heathcote Ball & Co Ltd [2000] 1 WLR 1962 **78, 94, 213**

Bertram, Armstrong & Co v. Godfray (1838) 1 Knapp 381 **164, 176, 216**

Boston Deep Sea Fishing and Ice Co Ltd v. Farnham [1957] 1 WLR 1051 **173**

Brinkibon Ltd v. Stahag Stahl und Stahlwarenhandel GmbH [1983] 2 AC 34; [1982] 2 WLR 264 **98, 108, 214**

Caparo Industries v. Dickman [1990] 1 All ER 568 **112, 118, 214**

Charles Rickards v. Oppenheim [1950] 1 All ER 420 **78, 81, 213**

Clark Boyce v. Mouat [1994] 1 AC 428 **178, 216**

Clegg v. Anderson [2003] 2 Lloyd's Rep 32 (CA) **78, 85, 213**

Dashwood (formerly Kaye) v. Fleurets Ltd [2007] EWHC 1610 QB **181**

Davis v. Sumner [1984] 1 WLR 1301 **7, 194, 209**

Dimond v. Lovell [2000] 2 All ER 897 **142, 146, 153, 161, 215**

Director General of Fair Trading v. First National Bank [2000] All ER 759 **16, 32, 33, 34, 209**

Donoghue v. Stevenson [1932] AC 562 **112, 117, 214**

Drummond v. Van Ingen (1887) 12 App Cas 284 **60**

Drummond-Rees v. Dorset CC [1997] CLY 967 **133**

Eastern Distributors Ltd v. Goldring [1957] 2 All ER 525 **64, 72, 212**

Egan v. Motor Services (Bath) Ltd [2007] EWCA Civ 1002 **56**

Emma Carey and others v. HSBC Bank and others [2009] EWHC 3417 QB **142, 156, 216**

Entores Ltd v. Miles Far East Corp [1955] 2 QB 327 **98, 107, 214**

Feldoral Foundry plc v. Hermes Leasing (London) Ltd [2004] EWCA Civ 747 **53, 210**

First Energy (UK) Ltd v. Hungarian International Bank Ltd [1993] 2 Lloyd's Rep 194 **170, 216**

Freeman & Lockyer v. Buckhurst Park Properties Ltd [1964] 2 QB 480 **164, 169, 217**

Grant v. Australian Knitting Mills Ltd [1936] AC 85 (PC) **58, 211**

Griffiths v. Peter Conway Ltd [1939] 1 All ER 685 **58**

Hadley v. Baxendale (1854) 9 Exch 341 **78, 89, 90, 95, 116, 213**

Hare v. Schurek [1993] CCLR 47 **150, 216**

▌Statutes

Statutory Instruments

■ European Legislation

The need for consumer protection

1

Revision checklist

Essential points you should know:

- [ ] Why consumers need protecting in commercial transactions
- [ ] The absence of a uniform statutory definition of consumer status
- [ ] How case law has extended definitions of consumer status
- [ ] How European law definitions compare with those in English law
- [ ] The extent to which commercial transactions can be regulated

■ Topic map

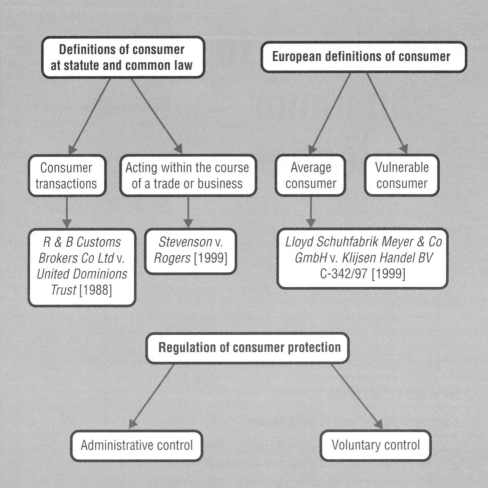

◼ Introduction

Because the consumer has the potential to be exploited by unscrupulous traders they receive greater protection from the law.

So, under the aegis of the European Union, the UK has increased regulation by introducing legislation, codes of practice and powers of enforcement by public authorities. By regulating transactions between business and consumers, most recent reform has indeed afforded the consumer greater protection, but these reforms also need to include small and medium-sized enterprises, so that they can compete on equal terms. Bear in mind that a customer's status in a commercial transaction will determine the level of protection given to them.

ASSESSMENT ADVICE

Essay questions

The question may take the form of a quotation upon which you are invited to comment. It is important to show, therefore, an understanding of the rationale behind consumer protection and why a party might prefer to achieve consumer status in a transaction. When describing various statutory definitions of consumer status, always highlight the potential loopholes in a definition by comparing and contrasting it with any other apt definition. Always use case law to illustrate how the courts utilise the definitions to reflect context, and take the opportunity to comment upon any discrepancies that may exist between the cases.

Problem questions

Consumer status issues in problem questions usually have to be interpreted alongside exclusions of liability for defective products or services, and will involve a detailed analysis of any effects that unfair terms legislation has on consumers and businesses, examples of which can be found in Chapter 3.

◼ Sample question

Could you answer this question? Below is a typical essay question that could arise on this topic. Guidelines on answering the question are included at the end of this chapter, whilst a sample problem question and guidance on tackling it can be found on the companion website.

'The consumer, unlike some classes with claims on public bounty, is everyone all the time.' (The Moloney Committee on Consumer Protection (1961))

In light of statute and case law on consumer protection in commercial transactions, discuss the above statement.

■ Definition of a consumer

There is no generic definition on how a consumer should be referred to in consumer law. Most common reference to the status of a consumer is in respect of a term that describes a behavioural relationship between suppliers and receivers of goods and services. Statutory attempts to give a definition of consumer status are often decided by such implicit phrases as 'acting in the course of a business' or 'dealing as a consumer'. While the Unfair Contract Terms Act 1977, s. 12(1) recognises a consumer only indirectly as a consequence of the trading behaviour that emerges from a transaction, the Unfair Terms in Consumer Contracts Regulations 1999, reg. 3(1) and the Sale and Supply of Goods to Consumer Regulations 2002, reg. 2 define a consumer as a natural person whose trading behaviour has a direct bearing on the commercial transaction. It might well be that because consumer protection is given by criminal sanctions against traders as well as civil remedies for consumers, a standardised definition has not yet practicably been found.

✎ EXAM TIP

When outlining the definitions given above, try to show your understanding of their meaning by citing everyday examples of **consumer transactions**. Then distinguish the later definitions by emphasising that the consumer should be considered a natural, rather than an artificial person, i.e. a company. It may be worth commenting on what the situation might be were a natural person to buy domestic goods which were for use within their trade or profession. This will show your awareness of the possible conflicts within the statutory definitions. A statutory definition is likely to change according to whether or not it confers criminal liability (Consumer Protection from Unfair Trading Regulations 2008) or rights to consumers (Sale of Goods Act 1979) or restricts the common law rights of traders (Unfair Contract Terms Act 1977).

KEY DEFINITION: Consumer transaction

This is a transaction whereby a consumer deals with another party who is carrying out their trade or business.

Of course, it is not always clear when a party is dealing as a consumer rather than in a business capacity.

 Make your answer stand out

The courts have discovered loopholes in the statutory definitions: notably when a commercial enterprise buys goods intended for part-business, or part-domestic, use. Now examine the connection between the terms 'consumer transaction' and 'acting in the course of a business'. In particular, compare and contrast the following two key cases which examine the notion of dealing in the course of a business to determine the existence of a consumer transaction. The decisions may indicate how, in borderline cases, dealing as a consumer applies to receiving, rather than supplying, goods. See Dobson (2004); MacDonald (1993); De lacy (1979).

The following cases illustrate that identifying a party as a consumer in a transaction may be problematic.

'Consumer transaction' or 'acting in the course of a business'

KEY CASE

R & B Customs Brokers Co Ltd v. *United Dominions Trust* [1988] 1 All ER 847
Concerning: consumer transaction

Facts

A married couple, who ran a private freight company, bought a second-hand car for their personal and business use. It soon became apparent that the car was unsatisfactory and not fit for its purpose, and so they sought a refund under s. 14(2) and (3) of the Sale of Goods Act 1979. In response to this, however, the defendants claimed to exclude liability under s. 6(3) of the Unfair Contract Terms Act 1977, stating that the contract was not a consumer transaction at all as defined by s. 12 of UCTA 1977.

Legal principle

The purchase of the car was merely incidental to the couple's freight business and in the absence of a regular course of dealing for just such a purchase, the court held that they bought the car as consumers.

KEY CASE

Stevenson v. *Rogers* [1999] 2 WLR 1064

Concerning: acting in the course of a business

Facts

The defendant, a self-employed fisherman for over 20 years, sold his boat to the claimant. But the boat was not satisfactory. The court had to decide whether the sale was carried out in the course of a business, in respect of the seller being a 'man of the sea', but not a boat salesman as such.

Legal principle

It was decided that the obligation to supply goods of satisfactory quality would be imposed on every trade seller, irrespective of whether or not they habitually supplied goods of that type, i.e. including a boat for whatever purpose a prospective buyer had in mind for its use, over and above the seller's. The sale was held to be in the course of a business because it was the defendant's business property that was being sold.

The definitions of a consumer according to UCTA 1977 and UTCCR 1999

There is some difference between the definition of a consumer given by the Unfair Contract Terms Act 1977 and that provided by the Unfair Terms in Consumer Contracts Regulations 1999.

Unfair Contract Terms Act 1977, s. 12(1)	The Unfair Terms in Consumer Contracts Regulations 1999, reg. 3(1)
A party to a contract 'deals as consumer' in relation to another party if – (a) he neither makes the contract in the course of a business nor holds himself out as doing so; and (b) the other party does make the contract in the course of a business; and (c) in the case of a contract governed by the law of sale of goods or hire purchase, or by s. 7 of this Act, the goods passing under or in pursuance of the contract are of a type ordinarily supplied for private use or consumption.	'consumer' means any *natural person* who, in contracts covered by these Regulations, is acting for purposes which are outside his trade, business or profession.

It is interesting to contrast the definition of 'consumer' provided by penal statutes such as the now repealed Trade Descriptions Act 1968. The following case gives an example of how the term 'consumer' was interpreted in a criminal context.

KEY CASE

Davis v. *Sumner* **[1984] 1 WLR 1301**

Concerning: definition of a consumer under criminal law

Facts

The defendant, a self-employed courier, sold his car, which he had used as a courier applying a false description to the mileage. He would only be liable for an offence if it could be shown that he sold the car 'in the course of a trade or business'.

Legal principle

It was decided by the House of Lords that the defendant had not committed an offence because he was not involved in the business of selling cars.

How, then, does one define a 'consumer' when dealing with exam questions?

 Make your answer stand out

If a question requires you to analyse the term 'dealing as a consumer', you could point out that because consumer protection is granted by criminal sanctions as well as civil remedies, a standard definition may not be practical. The courts might not be so willing to impose penalties upon defendants in criminal cases and, therefore, are less likely to award consumer status to the injured party.

The European definition

The European Union, while using a definition similar to that of the Unfair Terms in Consumer Contracts Regulations, has introduced the concepts of the 'average consumer' and the 'vulnerable consumer' into consumer law by implementation of the Unfair Commercial Practices Directive 2005/29/EC via the Consumer Protection from Unfair Trading Regulations 2008.

The average consumer

The concept of the average consumer in a European-wide context has to take into account the social, cultural and linguistic practices condoned in a state's consumer transactions.

The vulnerable consumer

Vulnerable consumers are those who are particularly vulnerable to exploitation and only receive protection should they belong to a targeted group who are unable to make reliably informed decisions on their own behalf; such as is the case with the young, old, infirm or credulous.

The European case law

In addressing the issue of how an average consumer might react to misleading commercial practices, the courts have looked at consumer transactions carried out by the average consumer in their particular social, cultural and linguistic context.

KEY CASE

Lloyd Schuhfabrik Meyer & Co GmbH v. *Klijsen Handel* BV C-342/97
Concerning: the nature of the average consumer's perception

Facts

Lloyd Schuhfabrik of Germany had distributed shoes since 1927 under the registered name Lloyd, after using various signs as trade marks. The defendant, Klijsen, had distributed leisure shoes under the registered name Loint since 1970, and in Germany, since 1991. Klijsen had registered its mark in the Benelux states in 1995 and also applied to register it in Germany. The claimants, Lloyd, opposed the application and brought proceedings against Klijsen under the German Trade Mark Act. Klijsen argued that there was no likelihood of confusion between the names Lloyd and Loint.

Legal principle

The German court asked for a referral to the European Court of Justice, which ruled that aural similarity between trade marks may create confusion in the mind of the consumer, and the greater the similarity of goods, the more likely it would create confusion. In assessing the likelihood of confusion, the court must consider the desire an average consumer has towards the values expected of certain types of goods. The court recognised that 'the average consumer's level of attention is likely to vary according to the category of goods and services in question'. Nonetheless, the court assumed that all average consumers buying shoes would approach their purchase with the same level of recognition.

✎ EXAM TIP

Concentrate on the difference between the definition of 'consumer transaction' as given by UCTA 1977 and the more natural definition provided by the UTCCR 1999 and its implications for consumer protection. Cite relevant European case law to illustrate understanding of the concepts of the average and vulnerable consumer and of how these terms rely on the product marketed and the context of any agreed transaction.

There is a difference between the UK definition of consumer and that introduced by the legislation emanating from Europe.

 Make your answer stand out

It is important to appreciate that the concept of the average consumer is not principled, but subject to the product marketed and context of transaction, as well as to any cultural practices held over consumer agreements. As for offering vulnerable consumers protection, assistance will only be given when the vulnerable consumer is said to belong to a targeted group. An example would be where a trader is selling toys to children or health products specific to the elderly. Should a vulnerable consumer belong to a group of average consumers, for example an elderly person buying general health products, then that consumer's reactions will be treated in the same manner as those of an average consumer (Twigg-Flesner *et al.* (2005) Para. 3.12, p. 41).

The European definitions of 'consumer' will be examined again when dealing with unfair trading practices.

📖 REVISION NOTE

Both the Unfair Commercial Practices Directive 2005/29/EC and the Consumer Protection from Unfair Trading Regulations 2008 are dealt with in more detail in Chapter 11.

Chapter 11 deals with criminal liability for unfair trading practices.

❗ Don't be tempted to...

Take care not to underestimate the importance of the 2008 Regulations. These regulations on unfair trading have replaced the Trade Descriptions Act 1968 and cover *criminal*, rather than *civil*, liability.

As the 2008 Regulations implement the Council Directives, it is interesting to make a comparison between the Directive and Regulations to see how far the definition of consumer given in the former matches that in the latter.

The European definition of consumer in the Directive and 2008 Regulations

Unfair Commercial Practices Directive 2005/29	Consumer Protection from Unfair Trading Regulations 2008
Article 2(a) 'consumer' means any natural person who ... [i]s acting for purposes which are outside his trade, business, craft or profession.	**Part 1, reg. 2(1)** 'consumer' means any individual who in relation to a commercial practice is acting for purposes which are outside his business.
Recital Note (18) ... this Directive takes as a benchmark the average consumer, who is reasonably well-informed and reasonably observant and circumspect, taking into account social, cultural and linguistic factors – but also contains provisions aimed at preventing the exploitation of consumers whose characteristics make them particularly vulnerable to unfair commercial practices. Where a commercial practice is aimed at a particular group of consumers, such as children, it is desirable that the impact of the commercial practice be assessed from the perspective of the average member of that group.	**Regulation 2(2)** In determining the effect of a commercial practice on the average consumer where the practice reaches or is addressed to a consumer or consumers account shall be taken of the material characteristics of such an average consumer including his being reasonably well-informed, reasonably observant and circumspect.
Recital (19) Where certain characteristics such as age, physical or mental infirmity or credulity make consumers particularly susceptible ... in a way that the trader can reasonably foresee.	**Regulation 2(5)** In determining the effect of a commercial practice on the average consumer: (a) where a clearly identifiable group of consumers is particularly vulnerable to the practice ... Because of their mental or physical infirmity, age or credulity in a way which a trader could reasonably be expected to foresee.

✎ EXAM TIP

Of course, as the Consumer Protection from Unfair Trading Regulations 2008 implement the Unfair Commercial Practices Directive 2005/29/EC, they are likely to be interpreted to give effect to what the Directive requires.

■ Regulation of trading practices

So far we have considered statutory control of commercial practices. Administrative control of commercial practices is exercised by certain public bodies, mainly in the area of criminal liability. These public authorities have been given statutory power to regulate traders.

Administrative controls

Public authority	Remit
The Department for Business, Innovation and Skills (BIS) replaced the Department for Business Regulation and Reform (BERR) on 6 June 2009	Review new regulations on business practice. Produce Codes of Practice for new regulations and deal with consumer policy issues like health, and communication via new technology
Office of Fair Trading (OFT)	Promote business compliance with competition and consumer law and the development of self-regulation. Powers to curtail the activities of 'rogue traders' and those who infringe legislation
	Monitor markets and recommend reform. Provide consumers with information so that they can make informed choices and encourage them to take disputes with suppliers to Consumer Direct
Consumer Direct	A government-funded advice service to ensure that consumers are fully informed of their rights. It also provides assistance in the form of letter templates for those who wish to pursue their rights
Trading Standards Departments	Operated by local authorities to enforce legislation on fair trading to protect the consumer and honest trader
Ombudsmen schemes	Cover a broad range of trading such as insurance, utilities and legal services. Have the power to order compensation to customer

Voluntary organisations

Voluntary organisations also contribute to regulation by promoting good practice and consumer rights.

Organisation	Remit
Trade Associations	Devise schemes and Codes of Practice to encourage high standards in trading. Many also offer arbitration services in disputes between trader and consumer
Consumer Associations	Campaign for fair dealing and publish materials comparing the quality of goods and services. By virtue of the Enterprise Act 2002, they can complain to the OFT for investigation

■ Putting it all together

Answer guidelines

See the essay question at the start of the chapter.

Approaching the question

The quotation invites you to examine the definition of consumer within a commercial transaction. Potentially the answer could cover a wide area, so it is best to limit discussion to a few relevant pieces of legislation. This should give the opportunity for more detailed analysis and criticism.

Important points to include

You should consider the following:

■ Why there has been a shift towards giving the consumer more protection within a trading relationship.

■ How various statutes offer protection by means of defining consumer status.

- Draw on the definitions in UCTA 1977, s. 12(1); UTCCR 1999, reg. 3(1); SSGCR 2002, reg. 2.
- Are the differences in the definitions significant? Consider whether the statute confers criminal liability, civil remedies or consumer rights, or restricts traders' common law rights.
- To what extent has the European concept of 'consumer' as defined in UCPD 29/2005/EC and CPUTR 2008 affected consumer protection?
- Are there any conflicting decisions in the case law that highlight potential problems in the degree of consumer protection offered?

 Make your answer stand out

Keep your answer well structured and refer to the quotation. Show that you understand the relevant sections of any legislation used and how they have been interpreted by case law. Use the case law interpretations to address the issue of degree of consumer protection. By covering recent European legislation you will show that you are up to date and innovative in your approach.

READ TO IMPRESS

De lacey, J. (1979) Selling in the Course of a Business under SGA, 62 *Modern Law Review*, Sept

Dobson, P. (2004) Exclusion Clause: Dealing as a Consumer, *Student Law Review* 43

MacDonald, E. (1995) In the Course of a Business – a Fresh Examination, 3 *Web Journal of Current Legal Issues*

Twigg-Flesner, C. *et al.* (2005) An Analysis of the Application and Scope of the Unfair Commercial Practices Directive, Report for the DTI, Para. 3.12, p. 41

www.pearsoned.co.uk/lawexpress

 Go online to access more revision support including quizzes to test your knowledge, sample questions with answer guidelines, podcasts you can download, and more!

Contract terms

Revision checklist

Essential points you should know:

- [ ] How to distinguish between a term and a representation
- [ ] The difference between express and implied terms
- [ ] Types of terms: conditions, warranties and innominate terms
- [ ] Terms implied by statutes and common law
- [ ] Unfair contract terms relating to business and consumer transactions

■ Topic map

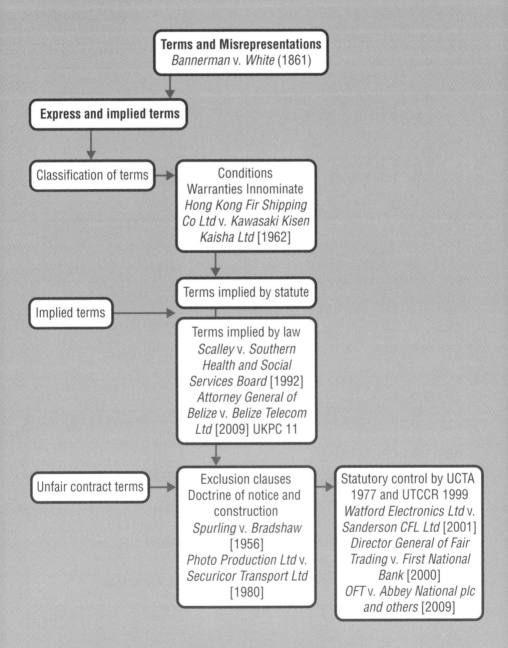

Terms and Misrepresentations
Bannerman v. *White* (1861)

Express and implied terms

Classification of terms

Conditions
Warranties Innominate
*Hong Kong Fir Shipping
Co Ltd* v. *Kawasaki Kisen
Kaisha Ltd* [1962]

Terms implied by statute

Implied terms

Terms implied by law
Scalley v. *Southern
Health and Social
Services Board* [1992]
*Attorney General of
Belize* v. *Belize Telecom
Ltd* [2009] UKPC 11

Unfair contract terms

Exclusion clauses
Doctrine of notice and
construction
Spurling v. *Bradshaw*
[1956]
Photo Production Ltd v.
Securicor Transport Ltd
[1980]

Statutory control by UCTA
1977 and UTCCR 1999
Watford Electronics Ltd v.
Sanderson CFL Ltd [2001]
*Director General of Fair
Trading* v. *First National
Bank* [2000]
OFT v. *Abbey National plc
and others* [2009]

A printable version of this topic map is available from **www.pearsoned.co.uk/lawexpress**

■ Introduction

Parties to a commercial contract will usually deal on standard form contracts, the terms of which may or may not have been negotiated.

Terms may be **express** (written or stated), or **implied** into an agreement. Sometimes you will find that a business is not always free to impose its own terms into a contract. For instance, terms may be implied into a contract by the court as a practical solution in the interests of business efficacy or fairness. In some cases, a term is implied into a contract by statute, where it may or may not be excluded or overridden by a business's own preferred term. Statutory regulation of terms is provided by the Unfair Contract Terms Act 1977 and the Unfair Terms in Consumer Contracts Regulations 1999. This topic lends itself to both essay and problem questions. In either case, you are expected to demonstrate an understanding of the need to balance the conflicting policies of promoting competition, while at the same time protecting the interests of the weaker party.

ASSESSMENT ADVICE

Essay questions
Should this topic appear in essay form, you would be expected to provide a critical analysis of the effect of potentially unfair terms in a standard form contract against both a business and a consumer.

Problem questions
A problem question will almost certainly focus on several terms within an agreement that could be a business or consumer transaction. As it is, you could be faced with potentially unfair terms and be expected to analyse their effect from the aspect of business and consumer. It is essential to demonstrate detailed knowledge of relevant sections of the Sale of Goods Act 1979, Unfair Contract Terms Act 1977 and the Unfair Terms in Consumer Contracts Regulations. In a commercial context, statutory regulation of potentially unfair terms needs emphasising, although the common law approach should be used to determine their reasonableness and effectiveness.

■ Sample question

Could you answer this question? Below is a typical problem question that could arise on this topic. Guidelines on answering the question are included at the end of this chapter, whilst a sample essay question and guidance on tackling it can be found on the companion website.

PROBLEM QUESTION

Mr Plant bought a shrub recommended by the Everlasting Garden Centre, as he needed a quick-growing, ground-covering shrub for the botanical garden where he worked. He used his trade discount card to pay for the plants. Those he had left over, he planted in his own garden back home. Unfortunately, the shrub turned out to be an invasive and vigorous variety of Japanese giant hogweed and has spread so rampantly that it has killed off other plants and even lifted up pathways, resulting in £5,000 worth of damage to the botanical garden and £1,500 to his garden. When Mr Plant complained to EGC, his attention was drawn to the following clauses on the invoice:

1 EGC agree to refund the purchase price of any products that fail to meet satisfactory standards of quality.
2 Subject to clause 1 above, EGC undertake no liability for damage, howsoever caused, by any product that fails to meet satisfactory standards of quality.

Advise Mr Plant on the effectiveness of the above clauses.

■ The difference between a term and a representation

Any pre-contractual statement made by one party to another may be classified as a term of the contract or a representation. A distinction should be made between the two because the remedies for breach of contract differ from those for misrepresentation. Breach of a term entitles the injured party to claim damages for **expectation loss**, whereas an actionable misrepresentation gives rise to a claim for **reliance loss**. This distinction becomes significant when examining sale by description in Chapter 3.

KEY DEFINITION: Expectation loss

Damages that aim to fulfil a contract by placing a party in the position they would have been in were the contract carried out, which may include loss of expected profits.

Of course, where expected profits cannot be ascertained or where no profit is expected, a party may wish to claim reliance loss.

KEY DEFINITION: Reliance loss

Damages to put a party back into a pre-contractual position in order to compensate for out-of-pocket losses.

Guidelines for determining the status of a pre-contractual statement

The writing test

Any statements written in a document are usually terms.

The skill or knowledge test

Statements made by the party with greater skill or knowledge are more likely to be *terms* whereas those made by the party with lesser skill or knowledge are more likely to be *representations.*

The time test

The greater the interval between making a statement and entering into a contract, the more likely the statement will be a *representation.*

The importance test

A statement that is significant to a party is most often a *term.*

KEY CASE

Bannerman v. *White* (1861) 10 CBNS 844

Concerning: the importance test

Facts

White, who wished to buy hops from Bannerman, asked him whether they had been treated with sulphur, emphasising that if they had, he would not be interested in buying them. Quite innocently, Bannerman said that they had not been treated, so White agreed to buy the hops. It turned out that sulphur had been used on some of the hops, thus White refused to pay. Bannerman sued for the price.

Legal principle

The defendant made it clear that he would not have entered into the contract if the statement had not been made. For this reason, the statement was considered a term in view of its importance to White. Clearly then, the term had been breached and so White was entitled to withhold payment.

The above case is an example of sale by description under the Sale of Goods Act 1979, s. 13.

KEY STATUTE

Sale of Goods Act 1979, s. 13(1)

(1) Where there is a contract for the sale of goods by description, there is an implied (term) that the goods will correspond with the description.

(1A) ... the term implied by subsection (1) above is a condition.

REVISION NOTE

Sale by description will be examined in greater detail in Chapter 3, alongside other terms implied by the Sale of Goods Act 1979. It is worth noting here that not every statement made during contractual negotiations will constitute a sale by description as defined in s. 13, which specifically refers to the implied term as a condition. For the classification of terms, see below.

Express and implied terms

KEY DEFINITION: Express terms

Express terms are terms that are written or spoken.

Classification of terms

Traditionally *terms* have been categorised as conditions or warranties. A **condition** is a stipulatory term which, when breached, allows the injured party the option to **repudiate** the contract and/or claim damages. A **warranty** is less stipulatory in the sense that when a breach occurs an injured party is only entitled to sue for damages.

KEY DEFINITION: Repudiate

A person shows by words or conduct that they do not see themselves as being bound by a contractual obligation. An example is where a person refuses to perform according to the terms of a contract.

This classification proved too simplistic, because a term can be breached in many ways with varying degrees of consequence. Given this, in certain situations a term can be classified as an *innominate* term. The following case illustrates how a term classified as a condition can have variable effects when breached and, as a result, can become innominate.

KEY CASE

Hong Kong Fir Shipping Co Ltd v. *Kawasaki Kisen Kaisha Ltd* [1962] 2 QB 26 (CA)
Concerning: innominate terms

Facts

A ship was chartered for two years by Kawasaki (the charterers) but was out of service for 20 weeks as it was declared 'unseaworthy'. The charterers mitigated their loss by commissioning a cheaper charter elsewhere. When the ship was declared seaworthy, the charterers repudiated the contract. The owners then sued for wrongful repudiation.

Legal principle

The charterers were in breach. 'Seaworthiness' was not in this case a condition, but an innominate term. It was neither a condition nor a warranty but the consequences of the breach were not serious enough to justify repudiation.

! **Don't be tempted to...**

It is not enough to state that a term is a condition, as the court may decide otherwise. A term will be seen as a condition in the following situations: where parties give themselves the right to terminate; where statute expressly labels a term as a condition (Sale of Goods Act 1979); or where the term identified as a condition can only be broken in one way.

Implied terms

Not all terms are expressed, some are implied.

KEY DEFINITION: Implied terms

Implied terms are terms that are not written or spoken, but implied in a variety of ways.

Terms implied by statute

Certain statutes imply terms, usually as conditions, into contracts. The Sale of Goods Act 1979 (see Chapter 3) implies the following terms into contracts for sale of goods:

■ The right to sell: s. 12.

■ Goods correspond with description: s. 13.

- Goods are of satisfactory quality and fit for purpose: s. 14.

- Where there is sale by sample, the bulk of the goods match the sample: s. 15.

The above implied terms are classified as conditions (s. 12(1) and ss. 13–15) or warranties (s. 12(2)). However, s. 15A allows a court to refuse to permit a buyer to terminate a contract for breach of a condition where the seller's breach is so trivial as not to warrant termination. *Note*: Any buyer (business or consumer) who has *accepted* the goods under s. 35 also loses the right to repudiate (see Chapter 5).

📖 **REVISION NOTE**

So far you have been given a brief introduction to the implied terms imposed by the Sale of Goods Act 1979 for the purposes of classification and rights of repudiation. It is important to be aware of ss. 12–15 when looking at the effects of the Unfair Contract Terms Act 1977 later on in this chapter. For further details on the sections mentioned above, you should refer to Chapter 3.

Terms implied by the courts at common law

Where terms are not expressed, they may instead be implied by custom as a matter of fact or in law. Terms are implied by custom usually to preserve recognised business practice. Should there be no customary business practice, terms may be implied by fact in cases where it is obvious that the parties intended such terms to be included and, as a consequence, were prepared to act upon them in *good faith*. Meanwhile, terms are implied by law in relationships of common occurrence, such as landlord and tenant. These terms do not necessarily reflect any intentions of the parties involved, but are seen as favourable duties for promoting their beneficial good.

❗ Don't be tempted to...

Take care not to overlook the debate on terms implied by law. There are one or two issues that pose questions. First, the debate between Lord Wilberforce and Lord Cross in *Liverpool County Council* v. *Irwin* [1977] AC 239. Whilst Lord Wilberforce stated that the implication of terms by law was by necessity, Lord Cross replied that the test should be one of 'reasonableness'. Lord Bridge in *Scalley* v. *Southern Health and Social Services Board* [1992] 1 AC 294 combined the two tests, stating that the implication of some terms into contracts was both *necessary* and *reasonable*. Secondly, there is a concern over the question of whether terms are implied or imposed by law. Unless they are excluded or modified expressly in a contract, some terms may well be imposed as obligations upon the agreement of parties.

KEY CASE

Scalley v. *Southern Health and Social Services Board* [1992] 1 AC 294

Concerning: terms implied by law

Facts

The claimant, who was employed by the defendant health authority, was not informed of his right to claim extra years on his pension scheme at certain favourable rates. As a result, he missed the deadline for exercising this right.

Legal principle

The duty to inform employees of such rights should be an implied term of an employment contract as it is a reasonable and necessary informative measure: '... it is not merely reasonable but necessary, in the circumstances ...' (per Lord Bridge).

 Make your answer stand out

It would be useful to draw the examiner's attention to Lord Hoffmann's recent consideration of implied terms in *Attorney General of Belize* v. *Belize Telecom Ltd* [2009] UKPC 10 (supported by the Court of Appeal in *Mediterranean Salvage* v. *Selmar Trading* [2009] EWCA Civ 531). In the *Belize Telecom* case Lord Hoffmann stated that terms cannot be introduced just to make a contract more fair or reasonable. What matters is what the agreement means to a reasonable person in possession of all background knowledge (reasonably) available.

KEY CASE

Attorney General of Belize and others v. *Belize Telecom Ltd and another* [2009] UKPC 10, [2009] 1 WLR 1988

Concerning: terms implied in law

Facts

The Belize government privatised their telecommunications service in 1989, transferring it to Belize Telecommunications Ltd. Under the company's rules there were three types of shares, Class B, Class C and a special share. Class B shareholders and the special shareholder could each appoint or remove two directors and the Class C shareholders could appoint or remove four of the directors. Additionally, the rules stated that, should ▶

a special shareholder own as much as 37.5% of the C shares, he could appoint or remove two out of the four C directors who made up 50% of the Board, as well.

The first respondent, Belize Telecom Ltd (BT) purchased the special share and 37.5% of the C shares from the government and then appointed two of the four C directors. Yet, to finance purchase of the C shares BT took a loan from the government, who retained a right to recover the shares in the event of a default. As it transpired, BT defaulted on the loan and so the government exercised their right to recover a substantial number of the C shares, but which did not include the special share. Subsequently, the government applied to remove the two directors that were appointed on behalf of the person who held the 'special share'. The Attorney General argued that, as the shareholding used to vote in the two directors (within the four) had now ceased to exist, the directors should leave. The company's objection was that the two directors could only be dismissed by a person holding both 37.5% of C shares, and a special share. The question put before the Privy Council was: did a shareholder with 37.5% holding of C shares have to own the special share, in order to remove the directors?

Legal principle

Lord Hoffmann's argument was that the directors could be removed, otherwise it would be absurd to allow just one nominee who had a special share status to block their dismissal, as the government were now in possession of 37.5% of the C shares. The overriding purpose of the appointment and removal of directors in this case was to ensure that the board reflected the shareholders' interest. There was an implied term that a director would vacate office when there was no shareholding to authorise their appointment.

■ Unfair contract terms

Terms have the potential for being unfair, especially when imposed by the party with the stronger bargaining power. As well as being subject to common law controls, unfair contract terms are also regulated by legislation. The Unfair Contract Terms Act 1977 is concerned with **exclusion clauses** operating within business and consumer transactions, whilst the Unfair Terms in Consumer Contracts Regulations 1999 refers to consumer transactions made upon a business's own *standard* terms.

KEY DEFINITION: Exclusion or exemption clause

A term or notice that attempts to exclude or restrict liability for one's acts or omissions.

Exclusion clauses

The common law approach to the control of such clauses depends upon the following:

- The doctrine of notice.
- Construction of the clause.

The doctrine of notice (incorporation)

This is a principle based on the assumption that a party is not bound by a term of which they are unaware. In order to ascertain whether or not a party is aware of a term, the court will assume:

- A party who signs a document will generally be bound by it.
- A party who lies about the effect of a clause may not be able to rely on it.
- A party will be deemed to have notice of a clause if it is within a document that a 'reasonable person' would expect to contain such a clause.
- A party may be bound by a clause if there is a course of dealing with the other party, or if the clause is *standard trade practice.*
- Any clause that is unusual or onerous is subject to the 'red hand rule'.

The red hand rule

When an onerous or unusual clause is seen to be unreasonable, it has to be highlighted, so as to alert anyone who may become subject to it.

KEY CASE

Interfoto Picture Library v. *Stiletto Visual Programs* **[1988] 2 All ER 348 (CA)**
Concerning: onerous terms

Facts

The defendants borrowed some photographs from a picture library. The delivery note stated that a fine of £5 per day, plus VAT, was payable for each photograph not returned by the deadline. It turned out that the defendants returned the photographs 13 days after the deadline, and thus received a fine of £3,783.50. But the court held that this term was extortionate and consequently reduced the amount to £3.50 per photograph, per week.

Legal principle

It is incumbent on a person seeking to enforce onerous or unusual terms to take reasonable steps to draw the other party's attention to it.

The following case gives a useful quotation from Lord Denning.

KEY CASE

Spurling v. *Bradshaw* [1956] 1 WLR 461

Concerning: the red hand rule

Facts

The defendant, who regularly dealt with the plaintiff, delivered eight barrels of orange juice to the plaintiff for storage in his warehouse but was not given a delivery note until a few days after delivery. There was a reference on the front of the receipt to conditions on the back, one of which was an exclusion clause for loss or damage caused by negligence of the plaintiffs or their employees. When the defendant collected the barrels, they were empty, and he refused to pay the storage charge, whereupon he was sued by the plaintiff. The defendant counter-claimed negligence on the part of the plaintiff, who in turn pleaded the exclusion clause.

Legal principle

Although the clause was quite onerous and as such should have been clearly shown to the defendant at the time of the contract, the defendant's claim that he did not receive notice of the exclusion until after the contract had been entered into was rejected as he admitted that he had received such notes in past dealings with the plaintiff.

This case is noted for the following dicta: 'Some clauses which I have seen would need to be printed in red ink … with a red hand pointing to it' (per Lord Denning).

Construction of the clause

Any clause that is ambiguous will be construed against the party relying on it – *contra proferentem* – to encourage clarity of expression. Against this, liability for a fundamental breach of contract can be excluded, as long as the clause clearly covers the breach.

KEY DEFINITION: *Contra proferentem*

In cases where a court determines a *term* to be ambiguous, a contractual interpretation will be construed against the interests of the party who insisted on its inclusion in the agreement.

KEY CASE

Photo Production Ltd v. *Securicor Transport Ltd* **[1980] AC 827**
Concerning: exclusion of liability for fundamental breach of contract

Facts

The plaintiffs contracted Securicor to provide security personnel for their factory. Securicor excluded liability for unforeseen loss from burglary, theft or fire, caused other than by negligence of their own employees. It transpired that a security guard did cause a fire, by deliberately throwing away a lighted match. In the event, the factory was destroyed, which resulted in a loss of £615,000, and yet the clause was held to be effective.

Legal principle

The parties were viewed as being on equal bargaining terms and free to apportion risk. Despite the fact that the damage was caused deliberately, the defendants had indeed excluded this very liability and were absolved from responsibility.

Statutory controls of exclusion clauses and unfair contract terms

Exclusion clauses are controlled by the Unfair Contract Terms Act 1977, whereas unfair contract terms imposed against consumers are regulated by the Unfair Terms in Consumer Contracts Regulations 1999.

The Unfair Contract Terms Act 1977 (UCTA)

UCTA 1977 restricts exclusions of liability for breach of contract and negligence by either declaring such clauses **void** or subject to a test of reasonableness.

KEY DEFINITION: Void

Has no legal effect.

The Act applies to **business liability** and consumer transactions, but not private transactions.

KEY DEFINITION: Business liability

Liability incurred by a person acting within the course of a business (s. 1(3) UCTA 1977).

KEY STATUTE

Unfair Contract Terms Act 1977, s. 12

This section states that a party deals as a consumer if he does not act in the course of a business with another party (who does act in the course of a business) and buys goods habitually used for private purposes.

☐ REVISION NOTE

The above section defines consumer status in terms of the transaction, rather than the individual, so there is nothing to prevent a business claiming consumer status when buying goods they are not accustomed to buying in the course of their own business. For problems arising out of this definition, see Chapter 1.

The table below outlines key provisions of UCTA 1977 with a brief explanation for each key section.

The Unfair Contract Terms Act 1977 section number	Explanation of section
Section 2(1): Negligence liability for death/ personal injury	States that no one can exclude or restrict liability for death or personal injury arising out of negligence
Section 2(2): Negligence liability for other loss	States that liability for other loss/damage arising out of negligence can be excluded if reasonable according to the guidelines given in s. 11
Section 3: Liability in cases of breach of contract	This section applies where businesses deal with consumers or another business on their own standard business terms, as where a business excludes liability for breach of contract and makes such terms wholly subject to the test of reasonableness

Sometimes a party dealing as a business may wish to exclude or limit liability relating to ss. 12, 13, 14 and 15 of the Sale of Goods Act 1979. The table opposite states that liability for s. 12 of SGA 1979 can never be excluded or limited, whereas liability under ss. 13, 14 and 15 can never be excluded or limited against a consumer, but may be against non-consumers if reasonable.

The Unfair Contract Terms Act 1977 section number	Explanation of section
Section 6: Sale and **hire purchase**	(1)(a) Liability arising from s. 12 (*title*) of Sale of Goods Act 1979 and (b) s. 8 of the Supply of Goods (Implied Terms) Act 1973 cannot be excluded or limited
	(2) As against a consumer; liability arising under (a) s. 13 (*description*), s. 14 (*quality and fitness for purpose*) and 15 (*sale by sample*) of 1979 Act and (b) ss. 9, 10 or 11 of the 1973 Act cannot be excluded or limited by any contract term
	(3) As against anyone *other than* a consumer any exclusion/restriction of the liabilities in s. 2 are subject to the test of reasonableness

Section 7 of the Act provides for other contracts under which goods pass from one to another, such as when goods are supplied with a service. As far as consumers are concerned, liability regarding correspondence with description or sample, quality or fitness for purpose *cannot* be excluded or limited. In cases concerning other dealers, then liability *can* be excluded or limited, subject to the test of reasonableness.

! Don't be tempted to...

Do not ignore the 'test of reasonableness' when attempting examination questions. Section 11 provides only guidelines, as opposed to rules, for assessing whether or not a term is reasonable. It is important to appreciate that whether a term is fair and reasonable will depend upon the circumstances which the parties ought (reasonably) to have known or thought about when the contract was made. Other guidelines in s. 11 include factors such as the availability of insurance when limiting, rather than excluding, liability. The case law shows that assessment of reasonableness can be unpredictable. Further complications result from the need to refer to Schedule 2 for exclusions concerning sale of goods.

You may find it useful to refer to ss. 12, 13, 14 and 15 SGA 1979.

⊞ REVISION NOTE

For descriptions of ss. 12, 13, 14 and 15 of the Sale of Goods Act 1979, see Terms implied by statute on pp. 21–2 above. Sections 6 and 7 UCTA 1977 effectively give much greater protection to consumers than to businesses, not just against exclusions of the implied terms granted under legislation for the sale, but also for the supply and hire of goods. Businesses often buy in bulk using generous discounts and, therefore, are not entitled to expect their purchases to be of the highest quality. Once more, this is reflected in the 'reasonableness guidelines' given in Sch. 2 to UCTA 1977.

KEY STATUTE

Unfair Contract Terms Act 1977, Sch. 2

Schedule 2 provides guidelines for assessment of reasonableness of exclusions in contracts for the sale, supply and hire of goods, by recommending that the following factors be taken into account:

(a) Strength of bargaining positions that allow for alternative choices available to the customer.
(b) Any inducements or discounts offered to the customer – bearing in mind a choice of purchase elsewhere – without the exclusion.
(c) Whether the customer ought to have known of the term, in the light of any trade, custom, or course of dealing.
(d) Does the exclusion come into effect when a condition is not complied with?
(e) Were the goods manufactured, processed, or adapted to special order for the customer?

The following case is a good example of application of the test of reasonableness.

KEY CASE

Watford Electronics Ltd v. *Sanderson CFL Ltd* [2001] EWCA Civ 317
Concerning: the test of reasonableness (s. 11 and Sch. 2)

Facts

A term in a contract for the supply of customised software excluded liability for indirect or consequential loss and limited liability for direct loss, to the price paid (£104,600). Actually, the software system was faulty and caused a £5.5m loss. At first, the exclusions were found to be unreasonable. But on appeal it was held that the clauses were, in fact, reasonable.

> **Legal principle**
>
> With regard to the exclusion of liability for indirect loss, it was agreed that there was equal bargaining power. Both parties were well aware of the term and its effects, and so the loss could have been covered by insurance. It was accepted that as a bespoke product, this was the only choice available. On balance, the clause was commercially reasonable as it 'limited liability' to the price of the product.

The Unfair Terms in Consumer Contracts Regulations 1999

 Don't be tempted to...

It is easy to confuse the 1994 with the 1999 Regulations. The European Directive 93/13/EEC on unfair terms in consumer contracts was implemented originally by means of the Unfair Terms in Consumer Contracts Regulations 1994. Some cases refer to the 1994 Regulations because these apply to contracts made between 1 July 1995 and 1 October 1999. On 1 October 1999, the Unfair Terms in Consumer Contracts Regulations came into force and in so doing, repealed the 1994 Regulations.

The aim of the Directive was to **harmonise** laws on unfair terms in consumer transactions, in order to facilitate trade between EC Member States.

KEY DEFINITION: Harmonise

> To make laws the same or similar.

 Make your answer stand out

Rather than create a single piece of legislation to regulate unfair terms, the UK government decided to implement the Directive separately so that there are now two pieces of overlapping legislation – UCTA 1977 and UTCCR 1999. Because this has led to complexity and some confusion, the Law Commission has published a draft Bill to unify the legislation on unfair contract terms (see Law Com. No. 292 (2005) Unfair Terms in Contracts).

Scope of the Regulations

The Regulations apply to unfair terms in standard form contracts as follows:

- Where one party deals as a business and the other as a consumer.

- Any disputed term must be one which has *not* been individually negotiated.

- If some terms *have* been individually negotiated, the contract may still be unfair if the rest of the terms are in standard form.

- Any terms that are incorporated in accordance with UK statutory or Community requirements are *not* subject to the Regulations.

- Terms that are **core terms** are *not* covered by the Regulations.

With regard to the terms themselves, they must be in plain, intelligible language and if there is any doubt about interpretation of a term, then the court will interpret it in favour of the consumer – *contra proferentem.*

KEY DEFINITION: Core terms

These are terms that either define the subject matter of a contract, or are concerned with the adequacy of the contract price.

Terms which have the potential to be deemed unfair

An unfair term is any term that is contrary to the *good faith* shown towards it, and thereby causes a significant imbalance against the consumer interest.

KEY CASE

Director General of Fair Trading v. *First National Bank* [2000] All ER 759

Concerning: the definition of a 'core term' and 'fairness'

Facts

The First National Bank made consumer credit agreements on their standard form contracts. One of their terms (a 'default clause') stated that should the bank obtain judgment against a debtor for default, then interest should continue to be paid at the *contract rate* until the debt was cleared. In the Court of Appeal, it was held that this term was not a 'core term' and that it was unfair according to the Regulations. However, the bank appealed to the Lords on the basis that it did not contravene the requirement of good faith, nor cause a significant imbalance to the detriment of the consumer.

> **Legal principle**
>
> The 'default clause' could not represent a core term because terms in contracts such as this had to be interpreted restrictively, otherwise a wide variety of terms could be seen as 'core'. Having accepted that the Regulations applied to the term, the Lords decided that the term was not unfair, since it did not cause a significant imbalance. The consumer had contracted to pay interest on the debt anyway, and should continue to do so until it was repaid.

It is interesting to compare the decision in *DGFT* v. *First National Bank* (2000) with that made by the Supreme Court in the following case.

KEY CASE

Office of Fair Trading **v.** *Abbey National plc and others* **[2009] UKSC 6**

Concerning: the definition of a 'core term' and whether or not the test of fairness can be used

Facts

In this appeal the Supreme Court was asked to decide whether the OFT could institute an investigation into whether banks' charges for unauthorised overdrafts were fair. In deciding this issue the Supreme Court had to decide whether or not the charges were classed as core terms. If they were core terms, then they were excluded from the provisions of UTCCR 1999 so the test of fairness could not be applied.

Legal principle

The charges for unauthorised overdrafts were part of the core terms of the agreement between the banks and their customers because they related to '… the adequacy of the price or remuneration as against the goods or services supplied in exchange'. The charges were deemed to be part of the price paid by the customer for the banking services provided. As such, they were not subject to the test of fairness because UTCCR 1999 did not apply.

Although the decisions in both of the above cases favoured the banks, it is difficult to distinguish *OFT* v. *Abbey National plc and others* (2009) from *DGFT* v. *First National Bank* (2000) in terms of how a core term is defined. Perhaps a distinction can be made on the grounds that a default clause operates only when a bank has obtained judgment against a debtor, whereas the unauthorised overdraft charges could be seen as an extra charge imposed by the banks at their own discretion. Besides, the justification given for defining a core term in the *Abbey National* case appears more substantial than that given by the Lords in the *First National Bank* case, although it does widen the category of terms that may qualify as 'core'. It may well be that if the charges had been found not to be a core term, and the test of fairness applied, then the court would be faced with the dilemma of having to decide whether it would be fair to pass the costs of compensating those who had been charged for unauthorised overdrafts onto those customers who kept within the limits set by their authorised overdrafts.

Schedule 2 UTCCR 1999 gives a non-exhaustive list of potentially unfair terms.

KEY STATUTE

Unfair Terms in Consumer Contracts Regulations 1999, Sch. 2

Here are a few examples of potentially unfair terms:

Where the seller/supplier, but not the consumer, can terminate the contract with or without reasonable notice; or, give himself, but not the consumer, the right to compensation for cancellation.

Again, should the seller cancel a contract and retain a deposit, or raise the price without giving the consumer any rights to cancel. On the other hand, a seller may vary a term for no good reason or for a reason outside the contract. Another example would be where the seller gives himself the sole right to interpret the terms of the contract, or ascertain just whether the 'goods' conform to the contract.

Regulation of the use of unfair contract terms

The Office of Fair Trading must consider all complaints unless they are frivolous or vexatious. Should they find that a term is unfair then they may apply for an injunction preventing the use of the term against consumers in standard form contracts. The Regulations give similar powers to Trading Standards Departments and the Consumer Association as well as to other regulatory bodies, like the Financial Services Authority (2001).

Comparison between the Unfair Contract Terms Act and the Regulations

Unfair Contract Terms Act 1977	Unfair Terms in Consumer Contracts Regulations 1999
Exclusion and limiting clauses only	All kinds of terms
Excludes insurance contracts; contracts for interests in land and auction sales	Excludes employment contracts; succession agreements; family law and setting up and running of a business; 'core terms'; and terms required by statute

Unfair Contract Terms Act 1977	Unfair Terms in Consumer Contracts Regulations 1999
Makes some exclusion clauses null and void and others subject to the 'test of reasonableness'	Applies the test of fairness to a clause on the basis of good faith and concepts dealing with significant imbalance
Protects business to business dealings as well as business to consumer dealings in contractual and non-contractual situations	It only applies to consumers who deal on the basis of standard form contracts with a business/trade/professional supplier

■ Putting it all together

Answer guidelines

See the problem question at the start of the chapter.

Approaching the question

Mr Plant has entered into a contract with the Garden Centre. The Garden Centre could be in breach of contract yet may be protected by the clauses. Identify the breach of contract first and then examine the scenario to see how the common law rules of notice and interpretation of terms apply before turning to the relevant sections of the Unfair Contract Terms Act 1977 and Unfair Terms in Consumer Contracts Regulations 1999. Finally, deal with the assessment of damages.

Important points to include

In identifying breach of contract, you should explain the effect of s. 14(2A), (2B) and (3)(a) SGA 1979.

Having described the relevant sections, you should then go on to explain the common law doctrine of notice particularly regarding signed documents and 'the small print'. Cases illustrating the effect of the *contra proferentem* rule may be applied to clause 2.

Then you need to explain and apply s. 6(2)(a) UCTA 1977 to analyse the effect of the clauses as imposed against a consumer. You may also mention that UTCCR 1999, reg. 5 will apply to classify the terms as unfair.

▶

In the event of Plant dealing as a business, s. 6(3) UCTA 1977 will need to be explained as well as the test of reasonableness as defined in s. 11 and Sch. 2.

Case law should be applied to determine reasonableness in light of the fact that clause 1 is a limiting clause.

Finally, in the event of the clauses being deemed subject to the test of reasonableness, the rules of remoteness of damage and measure of damages need to be explained and applied.

 Make your answer stand out

Structure your answer so that each point is dealt with in a logical sequence. Make sure you apply s. 14(2) and (3) SGA 1979 to the facts of the question. Address the issue of how the nature of the transaction affects the degree of protection offered by relevant legislation regulating unfair terms and how on occasion businesses have tried to assume consumer status in their dealings to take advantage of consumer protection. It is worth indicating that courts may show a more favourable attitude to limiting clauses imposed against business customers.

READ TO IMPRESS

Bradgate, R. (1997) Unreasonable Standard Terms, 60 *Modern Law Review* 582

Dobson, P. (2004) Exclusion Clause: Dealing as a Consumer, *Student Law Review* 43

Law Commission Report, Unfair Terms in Contracts, No. 292 (2005) Cmnd 6464

MacDonald, E. (1999) In the Course of a Business – A Fresh Examination, 3 *Web Journal of Current Legal Issues*

MacDonald, E. (2004) Unifying Unfair Terms Legislation, 67 *Modern Law Review* 763

www.pearsoned.co.uk/lawexpress

 Go online to access more revision support including quizzes to test your knowledge, sample questions with answer guidelines, podcasts you can download, and more!

Sale and supply of goods 1:

Implied terms

3

Revision checklist

Essential points you should know:

- [ ] What constitutes a contract for sale of goods
- [ ] The terms implied by the Sale of Goods Act 1979 and other related statutes
- [ ] How implied terms affect both purchaser and seller
- [ ] The degree to which liability for breach of implied terms can be excluded in both business and consumer transactions

■ Topic map

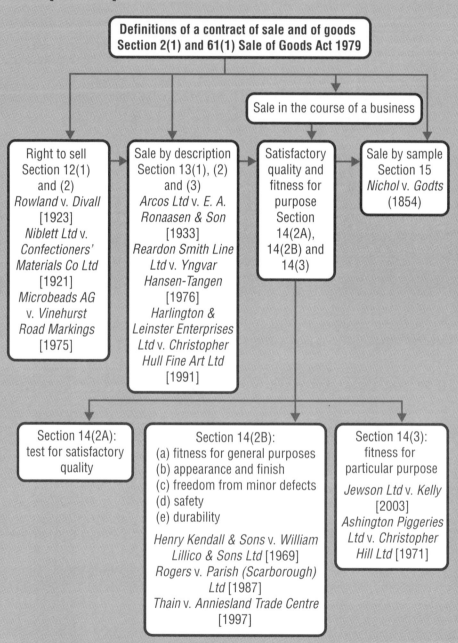

A printable version of this topic map is available from **www.pearsoned.co.uk/lawexpress**

■ Introduction

Students of commercial and consumer law need to be aware of the basic principles of contract, in order to understand the nature of a contract for sale and supply of goods/services.

Contracts that arise out of commercial dealing, whilst being subject to statutory regulation, are also underpinned by the principles of contract as developed through the process of common law. Therefore, for an agreement to have legal status there must be an offer that has been accepted in return for consideration, on the understanding that both parties intend the agreement to be binding. Usually parties in making a contract will have agreed terms. In any case, terms concerning title, description, quality/fitness for purpose and sale by sample will be statutorily implied into contracts for the sale and supply of goods.

In this chapter the statutory implied terms referred to in Chapter 2 are analysed in greater detail. Despite the fact that the emphasis is on ss. 12–15 of the Sale of Goods Act 1979 only, reference will be made to similar implied terms in other commercial statutes.

Then, at the end of the chapter, consideration will be given to the effect of exclusion clauses on statutory implied terms.

ASSESSMENT ADVICE

Essay questions

These may require an explanation and evaluation of the case law determining when a sale is a sale by *description*, or how the limitations on satisfactory quality operate. It is necessary to show a detailed knowledge of the case law as well as an ability to highlight and comment upon conflicting decisions.

Problem questions

Problems usually outline a scenario where a purchaser of uncertain commercial status buys goods that either do not match their description or may be unsatisfactory. Upon complaining to the seller, the buyer will be presented with an exclusion clause (or clauses) purportedly covering the buyer's *cause* for complaint. You will be asked to determine the liability of the seller and ascertain whether or not the clauses are effective.

■ Sample question

Could you answer this question? Below is a typical problem question that could arise on this topic. Guidelines on answering the question are included at the end of this chapter, whilst a sample essay question and guidance on tackling it can be found on the companion website.

PROBLEM QUESTION

Mr Plant needed a quick-growing, ground-covering shrub for the botanical garden where he worked. He bought a shrub recommended as 'quick-growing, hardy and compatible with other plants' by the Everlasting Garden Centre (EGC). Having used his trade discount card to pay for them, he still had some shrubs left over, and planted them in his own garden at home. Unfortunately, the shrub turned out to be invasive and toxic and has spread rapidly, killing off hostas and lifting up pathways, resulting in damage estimated at £10,000 to the botanical garden. Of course, he has also suffered damage to his own garden and what is more, his dog Fleur died after chewing a root. When Mr Plant complained to EGC, his attention was drawn to the following clauses in the invoice:

(1) EGC agree to refund the purchase price of any products that fail to comply with any description applied to the goods.
(2) Subject to clause 1 above, EGC undertake no liability for damage, howsoever caused, by any of their products.
(3) EGC undertake no liability as to the fitness for any specified purpose of any goods sold.

Advise Mr Plant on liability of EGC for:

(a) The botanical garden's loss.
(b) His personal loss.

Note: This question introduces a variation on the sample question found in Chapter 2.

■ Definition of a contract for sale of goods

Section 2(1) of the Sale of Goods Act 1979 defines a contract of sale of goods as one in which property is transferred from the seller to the buyer for a price.

KEY STATUTE

Sale of Goods Act 1979, s. 2(1)

A contract of sale of goods is a contract by which the seller transfers or agrees to transfer the property in *goods* to the buyer for a *money consideration*, called the price.

Consideration in contracts for sale of goods must be in the form of money, cash, cheque or credit card, and this makes them distinguishable from contracts of barter. Contracts of hire are also excluded from the definition, as there is no passage of ownership of property in such contracts.

Goods

Goods can be existing or future (s. 5 SGA 1979), specific, ascertained or unascertained. Existing goods are those which are owned or possessed by the seller, whereas future goods are goods to be manufactured or procured by the seller after making the contract of sale. Specific goods are those identified and agreed on at the time of sale whereas ascertained goods are identified and agreed on after the contract of sale has been made.

KEY STATUTE

Sale of Goods Act 1979, s. 61(1)

… 'specific goods' means goods identified and agreed on *at the time* a contract of sale is made (and includes an undivided share, specified as a fraction or percentage, of goods identified and agreed on as aforesaid …).

📖 REVISION NOTE

The distinction between existing and future goods, and specific and unascertained goods, is important in relation to the passing of property and risk as explained in Chapter 4.

Section 61(1) SGA also defines goods as 'all personal chattels other than things in action'. Therefore, goods must be tangible rather than intangible items.

'Goods' for the purposes of Sale of Goods Act 1979, s. 61(1)

'Goods'	Not 'Goods'
Tangible items that can be physically touched, e.g. a car, furniture, food, and severable items, such as agricultural crops	Intangibles, e.g. guarantees
	Contracts for the sale of land and non-severable items attached to land
	Contracts for labour and materials, e.g. commissioned works of art

Contract formation in commercial agreements

Entering into a contract for sale of goods is reasonably straightforward as there are no specific formalities.

KEY STATUTE

Sale of Goods Act 1979, s. 4: how a contract of sale is made

(1) ... a contract of sale can be made in writing (either with or without seal), or by word of mouth, or partly in writing and partly by word of mouth or may be implied from the conduct of the parties.

The common law requirements for formation of contract – legal intention, offer, acceptance and **consideration** apply.

KEY DEFINITION: Consideration

What each party gives to another in an agreement: usually the price for which a promise is bought.

Usually the price in a contract of sale is agreed beforehand, but occasionally the parties may leave the price to be fixed at a future date. The Sale of Goods Act 1979 makes provision for this in s. 8.

KEY STATUTE

Sale of Goods Act 1979, s. 8: ascertainment of price

(1) The price in a contract of sale may be fixed by the contract, or may be left to be fixed in a manner agreed by the contract, or may be determined by the course of dealing between the parties.
(2) Where the price is not determined as mentioned ... above, the buyer must pay a reasonable price.
(3) What is a reasonable price is a question of fact dependent on the circumstances of each particular case.

There is a similar provision in the Supply of Goods and Services Act 1982 (s. 15).

KEY STATUTE

Supply of Goods and Services Act 1982, s. 15: implied term about consideration

(1) Where under a contract for the supply of services, the consideration ... is not determined by the contract, it is left to be determined in a manner agreed by the contract or determined by the course of dealing between the parties. There is an implied term that the party contracting with the supplier will pay a reasonable charge.
(2) What is a reasonable charge is a question of fact.

 Make your answer stand out

The courts may not apply s. 8 SGA 1979 if they think the parties should have agreed a price. By not agreeing something as fundamental as the price, the court may determine that the agreement is too uncertain to be an enforceable contract.

KEY CASE

May & Butcher v. *R* [1934] 2 KB 17

Concerning: an uncertain agreement

Facts

In a contract for sale of tentage by the government, one of the terms stated that the price should be agreed 'from time to time' as the tentage became available.

Legal principle

This was considered merely an agreement to agree.

The decision in *May & Butcher* was based on the fact that the whole contract was uncertain. It was difficult to determine the intent of the parties. In a situation where price is a minor matter in respect of the other terms of an agreement, then the contract will still be enforceable, since s. 8 would apply.

 Make your answer stand out

Consideration can be viewed as evidence of legal intent. If so, then is consideration really a necessary reason to enforce a promise? Could other factors show evidence of legal intent or provide good reason to enforce a promise? These might include the behaviour of the parties concerned, deposits, or previous course of dealing.

Deposits as evidence of legal intent

A pre-payment may be made as either a deposit or part-payment at the time of making an agreement to purchase. Whether or not this pre-payment is evidence of **legal intent** will depend upon what the parties agree to. Where no agreement as to the effect of such a pre-payment is made, it may be seen as a *deposit*, which is generally regarded as evidence of legal intent and subject to forfeiture. Alternatively, if the pre-payment is seen as a *part-payment*, it can be recovered. However, this would be subject to examination of all the circumstances of the transaction.

KEY DEFINITION: Legal intent

Where both parties intend the agreement to have legal effect.

□ REVISION NOTE

Whilst a contract will be formed at common law only if there is offer, acceptance, consideration and legal intent, statutes like the Sale of Goods Act 1979 imply terms into agreements in order to regulate the criteria for governing a contract's stated aim. Where these implied terms are superseded by the agreement of the parties themselves, then the rules of the common law become stipulatory in any dispute.

Terms implied by the Sale of Goods Act 1979

In Chapter 2, ss. 12–15 SGA 1979 were introduced as examples of terms implied into contracts by statute. The mere fact that they are implied means that they do not have to be *expressed* in any agreement between the buyer and the seller.

■ Section 12(1) – it is an implied *condition* that the seller has the *right to sell* the goods.

- Section 12(2) – it is an implied *warranty* that the goods are *free from encumbrances* and the buyer can enjoy *quiet possession.*

- Section 13(1) – it is an implied condition that goods sold by description will comply with that description.

- Section 14(2) – it is an implied condition that goods sold in the course of a business are of satisfactory quality.

- Section 14(3) – it is an implied *condition* that goods *sold in the course of a business are fit for the buyer's purpose* (provided that it is reasonable for the buyer to rely upon the seller's skill and judgement in selecting goods suitable for that purpose).

- Section 15(2) – it is an implied *condition* that *where goods are sold by sample, the bulk will match the sample* and it is implied that the goods are *free from any defects*, which would render the goods *unsatisfactory*, if these defects would *not be apparent on reasonable examination.*

> **! Don't be tempted to...**
>
> It is easy to overlook the fact that whilst ss. 12, 13 and 15 SGA 1979 apply to all contracts for sale of goods, s.14 applies *only* to goods sold in the course of a business. Consequently, in the event of quality issues in private sales, the operative principle is one of **caveat emptor**.

KEY DEFINITION: Caveat emptor

Let the buyer beware.

The right to sell: s. 12

KEY STATUTE

Sale of Goods Act 1979, s. 12(1)

There is an implied condition on the part of the seller that in the case of a sale he has the right to sell ..., and in the case of an *agreement to sell* ... he will have such a right *at the time* when property is to pass.

When s. 12(1) is breached, the buyer has the right to repudiate the contract and claim a refund of the price, on the principle of total failure of consideration, even if he has used the goods for some time.

KEY CASE

Rowland v. *Divall* [1923] 2 KB 500

Concerning: remedy for total failure of consideration

Facts

A car was stolen from its owner (O) and the thief (T) sold it to the defendant (D). The defendant sold it to the claimant car dealer (C) for £334, who painted it and sold it to Colonel Railsdon (CR) for £400. Such a series of transactions can be illustrated as follows:

O (car stolen by T) → T (sold to D) → D (sold to C for £334) → C (sold to CR for £400) → CR

Having recovered the car the police restored it to O; upon which CR claimed £400 from C, who in turn claimed £334 from D.

Legal principle

It was held that C was entitled to claim back £334 from D because D's *cause of action* was against T, who in fact never had the right to sell, anyway. No one except O had the right to sell the car. Despite the fact that possession had been transferred, ownership had not. Furthermore, there had been a total failure of consideration.

! Don't be tempted to...

Take care not to confuse ownership with the right to sell. No seller needs to own property to have the right to sell it, as is shown when an agent does not own the property he sells, but does have the right to pass title to a buyer by selling it. Conversely, an owner of goods may not have the right to sell them, where by doing so, he would breach copyright laws. The *legal* right to sell and *transfer ownership* should not be confused with *ownership* (in itself).

KEY CASE

Niblett Ltd v. *Confectioners' Materials Co Ltd* [1921] 3 KB 387

Concerning: owners not having the right to sell

Facts

A company purchased 3,000 tins of condensed milk from the defendants. However, 1,000 of the tins were labelled 'Nissly' and the claimant (company) was told by Nestlé that if they sold these tins they would seek an injunction for breach of their trade mark.

The claimants took action against the defendants for breach of s. 12(1) because they were unable to sell the milk without removing the labels.

Legal principle

Section 12(1) had been breached by the defendants. The sellers did, of course, own the milk, but had no right to sell it because Nestlé, in owning the trade mark, were entitled to an injunction to prevent them from doing so.

Implied warranties under s. 12

Implied warranties as to possession are provided by ss. 12(2)(a) and (b) SGA 1979. The former states that the goods are free from any undisclosed encumbrances or charges, while the latter says that the buyer will be entitled to continuing undisturbed possession, unless by the time of the sale he was made aware of the rights of others over the goods.

KEY CASE

Microbeads AG v. Vinehurst Road Markings **[1975] 1 WLR 218**

Concerning: quiet possession of goods

Facts

This case concerns a buyer who purchased some road marking machines which, unknown to both buyer and seller, were subject to a patent application by a third party. The patent was granted after the contract was made whereon the third party sued the buyer for breach of patent. Thereafter, the buyer claimed against the seller for breach of s. 12(1) and (2).

Legal principle

Section 12(1) had not been breached, as the sellers had the right to sell the machines at the time the contract was made. With regard to s. 12(2)(b), the buyer was still entitled to continued quiet possession, without the prospect of an action for breach of patent by any third party. Of course, in this case the implied term had been breached.

Section 12(1) and (2) will not apply in uncertain circumstances where the seller contracts to transfer a title he does not necessarily possess. Nevertheless, s. 12(4) and (5) implies warranties of quiet possession that require the seller to inform the buyer of any charges or encumbrances known before the contract was made.

Sale by description: s. 13

Sale of Goods Act 1979, s. 13(1)

Where there is a contract for sale of goods by description, there is an implied condition that the goods will correspond with the description.

To what extent must the goods correspond with their description?

Formerly, goods had to match their description very closely, which was made clear in the *Arcos Ltd* v. *E. A. Ronaasen & Son* case, as outlined below.

Arcos Ltd v. *E. A. Ronaasen & Son* [1933] AC 470

Concerning: strict performance of the contract

Facts

In a contract to buy wooden staves they were found to be nine-sixteenths of an inch instead of half an inch thick. The buyer, who was looking for a way to avoid the contract as the price of timber had fallen, wished to repudiate for breach.

Legal principle

Although the thickness of the staves made no difference to their usefulness, the purchaser was entitled to reject the whole consignment on the grounds that the description did not match that given to the staves. 'A ton does not mean about a ton, or a yard about a yard ...' (per Lord Atkin).

Lord Atkin did say, albeit *obiter*, that the law will not take notice of 'microscopic deviations'. Later cases have tried to minimise the exercise of the right to repudiate in such circumstances. Also, ss. 15A and 30(2A) of the Sale of Goods Act 1979 now allow a court to refuse to allow rejection where the seller's breach is insignificant.

Goods are 'sold by description' when the buyer *relies* upon whatever that description implies. The mere fact that descriptions are attached to goods does not necessarily mean that they have been 'sold by description'. Obviously where goods have not been seen or identified (but have been described) they qualify as goods 'sold by description'. Again, specific goods that have been identified can also be categorised as having been 'sold by description'.

Reardon Smith Line Ltd v. *Yngvar Hansen-Tangen* [1976] 1 WLR 989

Concerning: limitation of the rule of strict performance

Facts

The respondents agreed to charter a tanker which was in the process of being built in shipyard *Osaka No 354.* The ship was, in fact, built in shipyard *Oshima 004.* By the time the tanker was built, the charterers were looking to avoid the contract and claimed that the contract had not been strictly performed because the vessel did not comply with its description.

Legal principle

The House of Lords held that the words describing the shipyard were used as a means of identifying the tanker, and were not meant to be a description of the ship and were, therefore, not a condition of the contract. The charterers were not entitled to avoid their obligations by repudiating the agreement.

 Make your answer stand out

In *Reardon Smith Line Ltd* v. *Yngvar Hansen-Tangen* Lord Wilberforce suggested that a sale will only be a 'sale by description' if the words used to describe the goods refer to a significant part of the *identity* of the goods themselves.

REVISION NOTE

Conditions and implied terms were introduced in Chapter 2. Often parties will look for ways to avoid their obligation; accordingly, the common law developed limitations to the rule of strict performance by applying to the rule precepts such as the doctrine of substantial performance, partial performance and divisible contracts. Likewise, the Sale of Goods Act 1979 contains provisions that restrict the right to reject for breach of a condition. These provisions are examined in more detail in Chapter 5, which deals with performance in contracts for sale of goods.

KEY CASE

Re Moore & Co. Ltd and Landauer & Co. Ltd **[1921] 2 KB 519**

Concerning: strict compliance with description

Facts

The sellers sold 3,100 tins of peaches to the buyers, who rejected them because they were packed in boxes of 24 rather than boxes of 30, as described in the contract. It made no difference how they were packed, as the overall amount remained the same.

Legal principle

It was decided that the buyers could reject the whole consignment, since it did not match the contract description.

 Make your answer stand out

In the *Arcos* and *Re Moore* cases the transaction was a business rather than consumer transaction and the parties were expected to have good reason to demand strict compliance with descriptions. This is especially important in commodity sales, where it is common for goods forming part of a bulk in transit to be sold on by one commodity dealer to another under the terms of a CIF (cost including freight) contract. Here strict compliance with description is very important, as a subsequent buyer needs to rely totally upon the description in the transaction documents. Even so, commercial law, in practice, tends to discourage the strictest of interpretations, as it is 'not concerned with trifles'. Indeed, the Sale and Supply of Goods Act 1994 introduced an amendment to s. 13 SGA by changing its status to that of an innominate term through s. 15A. As far as consumers are concerned, s. 13 retains its status as an implied condition, but not for business buyers where breach would be so trivial as to make it seem unreasonable for the buyer to reject the goods. In effect, under the present law this might reverse the decision in *Re Moore & Co. Ltd & Landauer & Co. Ltd.*

Reliance on the description

Not only must the description relate substantially to the identity of the goods, but the buyer must *rely* on the said description.

KEY CASE

Harlington & Leinster Enterprises Ltd v. *Christopher Hull Fine Art Ltd* [1991] 1 QB 564

Concerning: reliance in sales by description

Facts

Two paintings described as works by Munter – a German expressionist painter – were sold for £6,000. Both the seller and the buyer were art dealers, but the buyer was a specialist in German expressionist art. As it happened, the seller admitted to an employee of the buyer that they knew nothing about Munter's work. In any case, both paintings were fakes, and being worth less than £100, the buyer thereupon claimed the right of rejection under s. 13(1).

Legal principle

This was not a sale by description as the buyer had not relied on the description offered by the seller, and so was not entitled to reject the paintings under s. 13(1).

Description in sale by sample

A sale by sample is frequently a sale by description and s. 13(2) provides that if the sale is by sample as well as by description, the bulk of the goods must correspond with *both* the sample and description.

KEY CASE

Nichol v. *Godts* (1854) 10 Exch 191

Concerning: goods matching sample and description

Facts

Oil, described as 'foreign refined rape oil' was bought by sample. The bulk of the oil matched the sample but neither the sample nor the bulk matched the description. The oil was in fact a mixture of rape and hemp oil.

Legal principle

The buyer was entitled to reject the oil as not matching the description, in spite of its correspondence with the sample.

Self-service sales

Just because a buyer selects goods from a display in a shop, it does not prevent a sale from being one of 'sale by description'. When selecting items, buyers often rely on descriptive labels in order to inform their decision to buy (see s. 13(3)).

KEY STATUTE

Sale of Goods Act 1979, s. 13(3)

A sale of goods is not prevented from being a sale by description just because it is on display.

✎ EXAM TIP

An exam question on 'sale by description' may also involve issues of quality (under s. 14). Remember that s. 14 applies *only* to goods sold in the course of a business, whereas s. 13 applies to all contracts for sale of goods. It is useful to point out that the courts have often interpreted a sale as one of sale by description to give a buyer in a private transaction a remedy.

Satisfactory quality: s. 14

KEY STATUTE

Sale of Goods Act 1979, s. 14(2)

Where the seller sells goods *in the course of a business*, there is an implied term that the goods supplied under the contract are of satisfactory quality.

In the course of a business

Section 14 applies only to goods sold in the course of a business and s. 61(1) defines 'in the course of a business' as inclusive of the professions and the public authorities. Since there is no protection regarding the quality of goods given to buyers in private sales, it is important to distinguish between private and business sales in order to establish potential liability. In many cases it is easy to distinguish business from private sales, but disputes arose where businesses sold goods that were only peripheral to their customary business. However, these kinds of disputes were resolved in *Stevenson* v. *Rogers* (1999) (see Chapter 1 for details), in which it was held that sporadic sales that were merely incidental to the seller's business should be construed as sales 'in the course of a business'.

! Don't be tempted to...

Be sure to highlight the distinction between dealing as a consumer and acting in the course of a business. In *Stevenson* v. *Rogers* it was decided that *all* sales carried out by a business should be defined as 'dealing in the course of a business' under the Sale of Goods Act 1979, s. 14(2) for the purposes of civil law (see Chapter 1). Sometimes a business *buys* goods that are incidental to its commercial activity and is regarded as *not buying* 'in the course of a business'. Under such auspices a business is given 'consumer' status as a purchaser of goods. Now, dealing in the course of a business – for the purpose of *sales* – under s. 14 SGA 1979, has a different meaning to dealing as a consumer – for the purpose of *purchases* – under SGA 1979 and UCTA 1977.

KEY CASE

Feldaroll Foundry plc v. *Hermes Leasing (London) Ltd* **[2004] EWCA Civ 747**

Concerning: dealing in the course of a business and dealing as a consumer under UCTA 1977

Facts

A company wished to know whether it could rely on the protection given to consumers under s. 6(2) of the Unfair Contract Terms Act 1977, when it purchased a faulty Lamborghini car for the managing director's use.

Legal principle

The company could rely on this section of the Act, as it had dealt as a consumer, and could reject the faulty car, thereby ignoring the clause which excluded liability for 'satisfactory quality'.

📖 REVISION NOTE

Reference should be made to exclusion clauses covered in Chapter 2, notably s. 6. Under UCTA 1977, a company can be given consumer status, by virtue of the definition of consumer transaction given by s. 12. Whereas under the UTCCR 1999, a consumer is defined as 'any natural person, who, in contracts covered by these Regulations, acts for purposes which are outside his trade, business or profession'.

Agency

Were an agent, acting in the course of a business, to deal on behalf of a private seller, then the private seller would be seen as acting within the course of a business. Unless, that is, the buyer is aware of the seller's private status, or their attention has been reasonably drawn to it.

Limitations on s. 14(2)

■ Defects which are specifically drawn to the buyer's attention attract no liability under s. 14(2C)(a). Retailers often label goods as 'seconds' or 'special purchase' to alert customers to potential defects, albeit not 'specific'.

- Also, a buyer may feel the need to examine goods; in which case the seller will not be liable for defects which *ought* to have been apparent on examination (s. 14(2C)(b)). Of course, if the defect is latent, or difficult to detect, the seller will be liable.

- Lastly, where the sale is by sample, the seller will not be liable under s. 14(2C)(c) for any defects which would have been apparent on reasonable examination, even if the sample was not examined.

Satisfactory quality

A statutory definition of satisfactory quality is given in s. 14(2A) and (2B) SGA 1979. This was inserted by the Sale and Supply of Goods Act 1994.

Sale of Goods Act 1979, s. 14(2A)	Section 14(2B)
… goods are of satisfactory quality if they meet the standard that a reasonable person would regard as satisfactory, taking account of any description of the goods and price (if relevant) and all other relevant circumstances.	… the quality of the goods includes their state and condition and the following … (a) Fitness for all purposes for which goods of the kind … are commonly supplied (b) Appearance and finish (c) Freedom from minor defects (d) Safety, and (e) Durability.

✎ EXAM TIP

In consumer sales s. 14(2D) and (2E) extends the 'relevant circumstances' mentioned in subsection (2A) to include any public statements about specific characteristics of the goods issued by the seller, the producer or his agent, particularly in advertising or labelling.

Before this amendment, the word *merchantable* was used instead of *satisfactory*. Goods were of *merchantable quality* if they were of an acceptable standard and usable. For the goods to have been of an *acceptable standard* a buyer would have chosen to buy them, on the same terms, had he known of their condition. As regards *usability*, goods that were usable according to their description were considered merchantable. So where goods could be used for many purposes, but only one purpose was not up to standard, they were still considered merchantable. Thus, the *acceptability* test (which favoured the buyer) was used more often in consumer cases and the *usability* test (which favoured the seller) tended to be used in commercial cases.

As s. 14 is concerned with 'normal' use, the buyer is not required to inform the seller of any purpose he has in mind for use of the goods. This puts the seller in the position of having to hazard a guess as to possible uses the buyer may have for the goods.

KEY CASE

Henry Kendall & Sons v. William Lillico & Sons Ltd **[1969] 2 AC 31**
Concerning: goods usable within their contract description

Facts

Kendall bought animal feed for pheasants. Unfortunately, the feed was contaminated with ground-nut extract that proved fatal to the pheasants but not, however, to other livestock.

Legal principle

This feed was merchantable, because it was only *unfit* for *one* of its purposes.

Fitness for purpose for which goods of the kind in question are commonly used

Goods did not then have to be fit for all the purposes for which they were commonly used, but it would suffice for them to be fit for, at least, *one or more of their customary purposes.* Following the 1994 amendment, s. 14(2B)(a) seemed to imply that goods must be fit for *all the purposes* for which goods of that type are commonly used, irrespective of the contract being a consumer or commercial transaction.

Be aware of the subtle change in interpretation of s. 14(2B)(a). The courts, generally, seem to be showing a more protective attitude towards those who buy defective products in the course of a business.

Appearance and finish

The general approach to what extent appearance and finish play a part in assessing satisfactory quality is laid out in *Rogers* v. *Parish (Scarborough) Ltd* (1987).

KEY CASE

Rogers v. *Parish (Scarborough) Ltd* **[1987] QB 933**
Concerning: satisfactory quality

Facts

Rogers paid £16,000 for a new Range Rover, which suffered from a number of *minor defects* to the engine and bodywork. After six months' use, the claimant sought to reject the vehicle, on the grounds of 'unmerchantable quality'.

Legal principle

The car was not merchantable, owing to the cost and expected quality of the vehicle. The owner also had the right as well to take pride in his car's appearance.

Freedom from minor defects

The question as to what constitutes a minor defect that would render a product's quality unsatisfactory, is one of degree. A minor defect on a luxury item might make it unacceptable. Even then, much will depend upon the nature of the defect in respect of other statutory criteria such as a product's safety or inherent abnormalities. In *Egan* v. *Motor Services (Bath) Ltd* [2007] EWCA Civ 1002, the tendency of a car to 'deviate' to the nearside was held to be the result of its 'camber insensitivity' rather than abnormal steering, which was not defective enough for it to be deemed unsatisfactory.

Safety and durability

Safety and durability will be assessed not only according to the intrinsic quality of the goods, but also according to external factors which will probably be due to how the goods have been used. That being so, it would be unlikely that a buyer of a well-used second-hand car could claim unsatisfactory quality, were the car to develop a defect shortly after purchase.

✎ EXAM TIP

The assessment of satisfactory quality involves using an objective test that questions whether a reasonable person would necessarily think the effects of a minor defect were sufficient enough to make the goods unsatisfactory. Use cases to illustrate just how the courts have applied this test, using the guidelines given in s. 14(2B)(a)–(e).

KEY CASE

Thain v. *Anniesland Trade Centre* (1997) SLT (Sh Ct) 102

Concerning: expected durability of a second-hand car

Facts

The buyer paid £2,995 for a second-hand car which was approximately five years old and had an odometer reading of 80,000. When the car developed a fault in the gearbox after two weeks which rendered it uneconomic to repair, the buyer pursued a claim.

Legal principle

The court held that it was sufficient that the car was fit for use on purchase and that in view of the age and price of the car, the buyer assumed a risk of breakdown at any time. A buyer should reasonably expect a second-hand car to be durable.

Fitness for particular purpose

One may negotiate a sale knowing that certain goods are required for a particular purpose. Provision for such purchases is made under s. 14(3) SGA 1979.

KEY STATUTE

Sale of Goods Act 1979, s. 14(3)

Where the seller sells goods in the course of a business and the buyer, expressly or by implication, makes known –

(a) to the seller, ... any particular purpose for which the goods are being bought, there is an implied condition that the goods ... are reasonably fit for that purpose, whether or not that is a purpose for which such goods are commonly supplied, except where the circumstances show that the buyer does not rely, or that it is unreasonable ... to rely on the skill or judgement of the seller ...

Typically, this means that when a buyer asks the seller for advice on a particular use of goods, it is normally reasonable for the buyer to rely on the skill of the seller. There may be occasions, though, when it would be seen as unreasonable to rely on the seller's own skill or judgement as the following case exemplifies.

KEY CASE

***Jewson Ltd* v. *Kelly* [2003] EWCA Civ 1030**

Concerning: satisfactory quality and fitness for purpose

Facts

A property developer claimed that boilers he had bought to install in flats were unsatisfactory, because they did not work well in the flats. Although the property developer and the suppliers had discussed the suitability of the boilers for the flats, the property developer had not *relied* on the skill and judgement of the suppliers.

Legal principle

The suppliers were not in breach of s. 14(3) in this situation, since they had not been truly called upon for their 'skill and judgement' by the buyers, who had not relied on their expertise. Neither were they in breach of s. 14(2) because the boilers were not defective.

✎ EXAM TIP

'One of the important points that arises from the *Jewson* v. *Kelly* case is the distinction between s. 14(2) and (3). Under s. 14(2B)(a) goods that are 'fit for all the purposes for which goods of the kind in question are commonly supplied' will be seen as satisfactory. The boilers in the *Jewson* case worked, although they were not up to the buyer's required standard. Under s. 14(3) once the purpose for using the goods is made clear to the seller, then the standard of the goods to be expected is higher. Take the opportunity to point out to the examiner that in the *Jewson* case, the buyer did not make it clear to the seller the specific purpose for which he required the boilers.

Particular purpose made known to the seller

Any purpose for which goods are bought does not have to be expressed to the seller, since it can be implied from the way the product is sold. When a buyer, for instance, enters a shop to buy something for everyday use, it is assumed that those goods will be fit for the purposes for which they are manufactured and displayed.

KEY CASE

***Grant* v. *Australian Knitting Mills Ltd* [1936] AC 85 (PC)**

Concerning: breach of implied terms of quality and fitness for purpose

Facts

After purchasing some woollen underpants, Dr Grant contracted severe dermatitis, on account of them being treated with a chemical that had not been properly rinsed out.

> **Legal principle**
>
> A breach of the implied terms of merchantable quality and fitness for purpose had occurred. As to their fitness for purpose, Lord Wright stated that it was implicit in Dr Grant's act of buying the underpants that he needed them for a particular purpose and in choosing to purchase them from the defendants he had relied on their skill and judgement in selecting for the stock's wearable qualities.

On occasion, a particular purpose needs to be expressed by the buyer to the seller. In *Griffiths* v. *Peter Conway Ltd* [1939] 1 All ER 685, the seller of a tailored Harris Tweed coat was not liable to the buyer who, upon wearing it, also contracted dermatitis, as the buyer failed to make it known to the seller that she had an abnormally sensitive skin.

Reliance

Still, the buyer must rely fully or partially on the seller's skill and judgement when buying a product for a specific purpose.

KEY CASE

> ***Ashington Piggeries Ltd* v. *Christopher Hill Ltd* [1971] 1 All ER 847**
>
> *Concerning: partial reliance on a seller's skill and judgement*
>
> **Facts**
>
> This case is about the composition of mink food that was made up using herring meal, which contained a compound toxic to mink but not to other animals. Because the suppliers knew the herring meal would be used to make food for mink, quite naturally, the buyers claimed that the meal was unfit for purpose.
>
> **Legal principle**
>
> Obviously the use of herring meal, sold as an ingredient for mink food, was unfit for this specific purpose.

✎ EXAM TIP

> Take the opportunity to distinguish the *Ashington Piggeries* case from *Kendall* v. *Lillico*, where it was determined that the food was of merchantable quality, because it fulfilled one of its common purposes of being food fit for animals. The distinguishing factor here seems to be that in the *Ashington Piggeries* case the meal was described as *mink* food, yet in *Kendall* v. *Lillico* the product was *animal* feed.

Sale by sample: s. 15

Samples are often used in sales, but this does not necessarily indicate sale by sample. According to s. 15(1) SGA 1979, a contract of sale is a sale by sample where there is an express or implied term in the contract indicating that it is so. In written contracts it is easy to establish a sale by sample, but in oral contracts the intent of the parties has to be fully determined. Once it has been established that goods are being sold by sample, s. 15(2) imputes two conditions:

- that the bulk will match the sample in quality; and
- that the goods are free from any defects (making them unsatisfactory in quality) which would not be apparent on reasonable examination of the sample.

In *Drummond* v. *Van Ingen* (1887) 12 App Cas 284 Lord MacNaghten, when describing the function of a sample, stated that 'the sample speaks for itself'. Similarly, s. 13 states that when goods are sold by description they must, above all else, correspond with that declared about their content.

> **! Don't be tempted to…**
>
> Be sure not to overlook the buyer's obligation to examine the sample. While s. 14 does not require the buyer to examine goods for satisfactory quality, s. 15(2)(c) makes such an examination of a *sample* obligatory. Once again, this is reinforced by s. 14(2C)(c), which allows the seller an *escape liability* for defects in samples that would have been apparent on reasonable examination of the sample.

Implied terms in contracts other than sale of goods

The implied terms in ss. 12–15 SGA 1979 have been extended into contracts of **hire purchase**, and supply of goods and services.

> **KEY DEFINITION: Hire purchase**
>
> A person, otherwise known as a bailee, agrees to hire goods on credit terms for a fixed period of time, with an option to buy (for a nominal fee) at the end of the agreed period.

The Supply of Goods and Services Act 1982 provides for three types of contract:

- Contracts for the transfer of goods (where goods are supplied with services).
- Contracts of hire.
- Contracts for services.

See the topic map at the beginning of this chapter for an outline of these implied terms.

Exclusion of implied terms

Whether or not the implied terms referred to in this chapter can be excluded depends upon the status of the buyer, and the effects of the Unfair Contract Terms Act 1977 and the Unfair Terms in Consumer Contracts Regulations 1999.

📖 **REVISION NOTE**

As you are expected to analyse the effects of excluding liability for obligations under the Sale of Goods Act 1979, you are advised to refer to the Unfair Contract Terms Act 1977, ss. 6, 11, 12 and Sch. 2 in Chapter 2.

■ Putting it all together

Answer guidelines

See the problem question at the start of the chapter.

Approaching the question

Mr Plant has entered into a contract with the Garden Centre. The Garden Centre could be in breach of contract yet may be protected by the clauses.

Important points to include

- Have any of the implied terms of the SGA 1979 been breached?
- Is this a sale by description?
- Is the shrub fit for a specific purpose? Does it need to be?
- What are the effects of the clauses under ss. 2(2) and 6 of UCTA 1977?
- What are the likely effects of the clauses upon a business transaction?
- Consider the test of reasonableness under s. 11 and Sch. 2.
- Explain the effects of the clauses upon a consumer transaction.
- What would be the effect of the UTCCR 1999?
- Address the question of damages, assessment of loss and remoteness of damage.

▶

Make your answer stand out

The fact that Mr Plant works at a botanical garden raises the question of whose skill and judgement he relied upon when making his purchases. You need to consider what facts would render the shrubs unsatisfactory. For example, they satisfy some of the descriptive criteria but are not compatible with another type of plant. Is the shrub fit for Mr Plant's intended purpose and fit for 'normal' use? Does the fact that the shrub is incompatible with one type of plant make it usable within its description? You should address the issue of buying as a consumer and as a business to highlight the greater protection offered to consumer buyers. What are the effects of the disclaimer clauses in terms of the loss suffered by the botanical gardens as a business, as well as Mr Plant as a consumer? Are any of the damages too remote?

READ TO IMPRESS

Bridge, M. (1995) The Sale and Supply of Goods Act 1994, *Journal of Business Law* 398

Ervine, W. C. H. (2004) Satisfactory Quality: What Does it Mean? *Journal of Business Law* 684

Hedley, S. (1996) Fitness for a Buyer's Particular Purpose, 4 *Web Journal of Current Legal Issues*

www.pearsoned.co.uk/lawexpress

 Go online to access more revision support including quizzes to test your knowledge, sample questions with answer guidelines, podcasts you can download, and more!

Sale and supply of goods 2:

Transfer of property and risk

4

Revision checklist

Essential points you should know:

- [ ] The circumstances under which property passes
- [ ] When risk is transferred
- [ ] Reservation of title
- [ ] Exceptions to the rule of *nemo dat quod non habet*

◼ Topic map

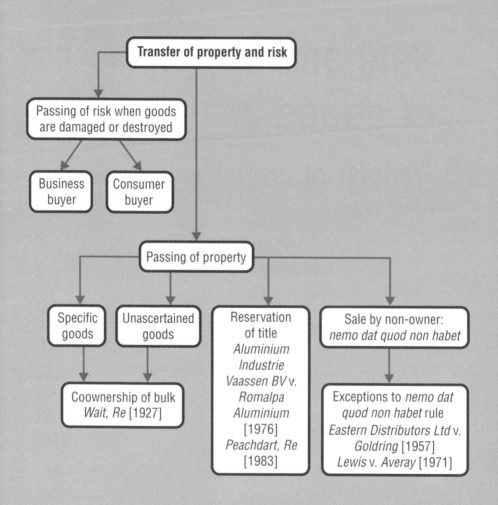

■ Introduction

Parties to a contract for sale of goods often agree to their own standard terms for covering precepts like the transfer of ownership, and the allocation of risk.

Whenever there is inadequate provision for these matters, the Sale of Goods Act 1979 will imply appropriate terms into a contract anyway.

ASSESSMENT ADVICE

Essay questions

These could focus on one aspect of transfer of title, such as reservation of title, and would expect you to demonstrate detailed knowledge of the case law.

Problem questions

Problems may present a scenario or series of scenarios covering several aspects of transfer of property. You will be expected to show a detailed knowledge of relevant sections of the Sale of Goods Act 1979 as well as the common law.

■ Sample question

Could you answer this question? Below is a typical essay question that could arise on this topic. Guidelines on answering the question are included at the end of this chapter, whilst a sample problem question and guidance on tackling it can be found on the companion website.

ESSAY QUESTION

Explain the effect of a **reservation of title clause** against a non-paying customer in the following situations:

(a) Where the customer has gone into liquidation.
(b) Where the customer has used the product to manufacture goods, which have been sold.

■ Transfer of property and risk

It is important to ascertain just when property passes, because risk normally passes with property. Exactly who bears the risk when goods are destroyed, or parties become insolvent, will determine whosoever suffers the loss. The parties mostly agree amongst themselves when property and risk passes from seller to buyer, by inserting clauses – such as a *force majeure* **clause** – into their contracts. Should they fail to do so the Sale of Goods Act 1979 applies.

KEY DEFINITION: *Force majeure* clause

A clause which allocates risk in the event of something that might happen.

 Make your answer stand out

You could point out that it is customary in commercial agreements for parties to make provision, with *force majeure* **clauses,** for what could happen should a particular event arise. These clauses will be effective only if they cover the event. Even then, they may not be enforceable if the predictable event causes exceptional and extensive losses: except where it can be shown that any loss was, in all probability, likely to occur. In maritime agreements it is common practice to include such clauses to cover the perils of the sea because the Law Reform (Frustrated Contracts) Act 1943 – which deals with division of loss – excludes carriage of goods by sea as well as transport of perishable goods. In effect, this means that the parties should ideally make their own provision for allocation of risk because if they don't, s. 20 of the Sale of Goods Act 1979 will apply.

KEY STATUTE

Sale of Goods Act 1979, s. 20 (passing of risk)

(1) Unless otherwise agreed, the goods remain at the seller's risk until the property in them is transferred to the buyer ...

The section goes on to say that property may transfer to the buyer before delivery.

The passing of risk when goods are damaged or destroyed

Business buyers

In the absence of an agreement between buyer and seller, s. 20 SGA 1979 states that the *risk* stays with the seller until property is transferred. The owner has **title or a right of ownership**.

KEY DEFINITION: Title or a right of ownership

An owner has exclusive rights and control over their property. The property in the goods is an example of a right of ownership.

! Don't be tempted to...

Don't confuse the terms 'ownership' and 'possession'. Possession is not the same concept as ownership. Suppose a right of ownership transfers *before the buyer possesses* the goods, the buyer would then have to bear the risk of loss of those goods even though they are in the seller's possession. For this reason, in a business sale, *risk passes with transfer of property in the goods (or rights of ownership)* whether or not the goods have been delivered to the buyer.

Consumer buyers

The Sale and Supply of Goods to Consumers Regulations 2002 instituted s. 20(4) SGA 1979 to ensure that goods remain at the *seller's risk* until the seller has *delivered the goods* to the buyer.

■ The passing of property

The point at which property passes depends on whether the goods are *specific*, or **unascertained**.

KEY STATUTE

Sale of Goods Act 1979

Section 61 defines 'specific goods' as: ... goods identified and agreed on at the time a contract of sale is made.

KEY DEFINITION: Unascertained goods

Any goods that have not been identified and agreed upon at the time of the contract are considered to be unascertained, including those chosen from an identified bulk.

Remember, **ascertained goods** are those that are 'earmarked' for allocation to a purchaser after the contract of sale.

KEY DEFINITION: Ascertained goods

Goods can become ascertained once they have been identified and agreed upon, after the contract of sale.

In Chapter 3 specific goods were distinguished from ascertained goods on the grounds that specific goods were identified and agreed upon before or at the time of sale.

The passing of property in specific goods

According to s. 17(1), property in specific goods passes when the parties intend it to pass. A person's intention is determined by their behaviour towards the terms of a contract. How a person's intention is to be determined is governed by the rules in s. 18.

Rules to determine intent in the sale of goods in s. 18

Rule number	When property passes to the buyer
Rule 1: Specific goods unconditionally sold in a deliverable state, even where time of delivery and payment are postponed	At the time of the contract
Rule 2: Specific goods sold on condition they are made deliverable by the seller	When the goods have been made deliverable
Rule 3: Where specific goods have to be weighed, measured or tested by the seller to find the price	Once goods have been weighed, measured or tested and the buyer has been informed of this
Rule 4: Where specific goods are sold on approval or on a sale-or-return basis	When the buyer signifies approval; does an act which adopts the transaction; keeps the goods for longer than the time limit fixed by the contract or for longer than a reasonable time

The passing of property in unascertained goods

Property in the goods cannot pass according to s. 16L until the goods have been ascertained. Where the buyer and seller fail to mention when property passes, s. 18, rule 5 applies.

Rule number	When property passes to the buyer
Rule 5: Goods must match the contract description, be ready for delivery and have been unconditionally appropriated to the contract either by the buyer with the assent of the seller, or by the seller with the assent of the buyer	Once the goods in a deliverable state have been identified and earmarked for a particular buyer

Ascertainment by exhaustion

This rule, which emanates from the decision in *Karlshamns Oljefabriker* v. *Eastport Navigation Corp.* [1982] 1 All ER 208, was inserted into SGA 1979 by the Sale of Goods (Amendment) Act 1995 and applies when a buyer may have ordered, say, 100 bottles of wine from a batch of 500, but out of which 400 have already been sold. As long as the remaining 100 bottles of wine are in a deliverable state, they will become *ascertained by exhaustion*.

Co-ownership of a bulk

Another reform introduced by SG(A)A 1994, via ss. 20A and 20B SGA 1979 was the concept of *co-ownership* of a bulk. A necessary reform was needed in light of the unfair decision of the *Re Wait* (1927) case.

KEY CASE

Re Wait [1927] 1 Ch 606

Concerning: ascertainment by appropriation

Facts

Wait bought 1,000 tons of wheat that was loaded on a ship on 20 November. The next day, he contracted to sell 500 tons of the bulk to X, who paid Wait for the consignment on 5 February. However, by the time the ship arrived on 28 February Wait had been declared a bankrupt, four days earlier. In the changed circumstances, Wait's trustee in bankruptcy now claimed the entire load of 1,000 tons on behalf of preferred creditors.

Legal principle

Wait's trustee was entitled to the entire load, whereas X was not entitled to the 500 tons he had bought, as it had not been appropriated (separated from the bulk), so enabling property to pass, even though he had paid for the goods.

Now, s. 20A allows a buyer who has bought a specified quantity from an identified bulk to become *co-owner* of a share of the whole bulk along with other co-owners, as long as a specified amount has been paid for out of an identified bulk. If all of the bulk is destroyed, the whole of the buyer's as well as the seller's share is destroyed. If part of the bulk is destroyed then the seller's share is destroyed first and the remaining co-owners will be entitled to a share proportionate to the price they have paid. Taking *Re Wait* as an example, s. 20A would have allowed X to become a 50% owner of the wheat, the remainder to be allocated to Wait's trustee.

Reservation of title clauses

Reservation of title clauses provide the seller with the power to retain ownership of the goods until they have been paid for by the buyer. Were the buyer to become insolvent before paying for the goods, the seller has the right to retrieve them. The goods remain the buyer's property, without any clause being in place, and will be seized by the liquidator and sold off to pay creditors. Retention of title clauses are often referred to as **Romalpa clauses** due to the following case.

KEY CASE

Aluminium Industrie Vaassen BV v. Romalpa Aluminium **[1976] 1 WLR 676**
Concerning: reservation of title in unmixed goods

Facts

In this case, AIV sold aluminium foil to Romalpa. The contract of sale included a clause which stated that ownership of the foil would not pass until it had been paid for, and were the foil to be mixed with other products during manufacture, AIV would become owner of the finished product and property in the finished product would not pass until Romalpa had paid for the foil. It also stated that any unmixed foil should be stored separately from products made with the foil and that Romalpa could sell these products on condition that AIV could claim money from the proceeds of the sale. This had the effect of imposing upon Romalpa a fiduciary duty to the sellers. When Romalpa became insolvent before paying fully for the foil, AIV claimed for the unsold foil as well as the proceeds of the sale of the unmixed foil.

Legal principle

As regards the unmixed goods, the clause had reserved title for the sellers who owned the unsold foil, and were also entitled to the proceeds of sale of the unmixed foil. AIV decided not to claim for the proceeds of sale of the 'mixed goods'.

Mixed goods

It is easy to enforce a clearly worded reservation of title clause over goods that are in their original state, as ownership will not pass until payment of price. More often than not goods used in a manufacturing process have their identity changed. Despite the reservation of title clause, property will pass to the buyer, since it is impractical to separate identity of the goods from the finished product. Instead, the courts are inclined to regard reservation of title clauses as a way of establishing a 'charge' that must be properly registered, so as to become security for payment for the goods.

KEY CASE

Re Peachdart [1983] 3 All ER 204

Concerning: the effect of retention of title over mixed goods

Facts

While the sellers of leather for manufacture (into handbags) could reserve title in the leather supplied, they could not reserve title in the finished product. Once made into handbags, the leather changed its identity. The reservation of title clause created a 'property right' as a charge over the handbags and in order to be effective it should have been properly registered under the Companies Act 1985, s. 395.

Legal principle

As the sellers had failed to register the clause as a *charge*, they were unable to recover either the bags or the proceeds of sale of the bags.

Sale by person who is not the owner

The provisions covering such sales are contained in s. 21 SGA 1979.

KEY STATUTE

Sale of Goods Act 1979, s. 21

Subject to this Act, where goods are sold by a person who is not the owner, and who does not sell them under the authority or with the consent of the owner, the buyer acquires no better title to the goods than the seller had, unless the owner of the goods is by his conduct precluded from denying the seller's authority to sell.

KEY DEFINITION: *Nemo dat quod non habet*

No one can sell what he does not have.

Only if a seller owns or has the right to sell goods at the time of sale can ownership be passed to a buyer. Otherwise known as the ***nemo dat quod non habet*** rule, which usually applies when a buyer purchases stolen property from a thief to enable the property to be recovered and restored to its true owner. To protect an innocent purchaser, the following exceptions to the rule are listed below.

Exceptions to the *nemo dat quod non habet* rule

Estoppel

Estoppel applies where the true owner acts as though the seller has the right to sell. SGA 1979 does not mention estoppel but implies it with the words 'unless the owner of the goods is by his conduct precluded from denying the seller's authority to sell'.

KEY CASE

***Eastern Distributors Ltd* v. *Goldring* [1957] 2 All ER 525**

Concerning: estoppel as an exception to the 'nemo dat' *rule*

Facts

M wished to buy a car on HP terms so he persuaded C to pretend to be the owner of M's van, and C sold the van to a finance company who supplied the finance for M to purchase the van. The finance was to be used to pay for the van and the car. When the deal to purchase the car did not materialise, M told C the whole deal was off and sold the van to Goldring who bought it in good faith. M failed to pay the hire purchase instalments for the van and so the claimants sued Goldring for the van or its value.

Legal principle

M was estopped from denying that C had the right to sell the car so M's title passed to the claimants who could recover the car.

Agency

An agent who sells a principal's goods with actual or implied authority passes 'good title' on to an innocent buyer. *Note*: Section 21(1) also recognises ostensible or apparent authority of an agent.

Mercantile agents

A mercantile agent can pass title of goods to a buyer without the authority of the owner (s. 2(1) Factors Act 1889). Section 21(2) SGA 1979 states that nothing in the SGA will affect the Factors Act 1889.

Authority of law

The law allows pawnbrokers to sell goods pledged to them as security for a loan, where a loan has not been repaid. See s. 21(2) SGA 1979, which allows special powers of sale in such circumstances.

Sale by person with voidable title

In cases where a thief has bought goods by deception from a seller who has not taken reasonable steps to check their identity and sells them on to an innocent purchaser, the innocent purchaser will be allowed to retain title to the goods. This is covered by s. 23 SGA 1979: 'When the seller of goods has voidable title to them, but his title has not been avoided at the time of the sale, the buyer acquires good title to the goods, provided he buys them in good faith and without notice of the seller's defect of title.'

KEY CASE

Lewis v. *Averay* **[1971] 3 All ER 907**

Concerning: sale under a voidable title

Facts

A rogue impersonated a famous actor in order to buy a car with a bad cheque. Before the car owner discovered the fraudulent misrepresentation, the rogue had sold the car on to the defendant who was an honest purchaser.

Legal principle

The Court of Appeal held that the defendant obtained good title because the claimant had failed to avoid the contract before the car was sold on.

 Make your answer stand out

All of the exceptions to the *nemo dat quod non habet* rule require that the purchaser who claims good title must have acted in good faith. According to s. 23 SGA 1979, the burden of proving lack of good faith rests with the original owner, whereas with the other exceptions the burden of proving good faith lies with the person who claims to have acquired good title.

Sale by a seller in possession of goods

This happens when a seller sells previously sold but uncollected goods to a second buyer. Section 24 SGA 1979 states that in such a situation the second buyer will gain ownership of the goods.

Sale by a buyer in possession of goods

A buyer in possession of goods purchased may sell them on to a third party with the original seller's (i.e. owner's) consent. See s. 25(1) SGA 1979, which applies when a buyer in such a position delivers the goods or title documents to a third party acting in good faith so the buyer can pass good title as if he was acting as a mercantile agent.

✎ EXAM TIP

It is useful to point out that it is not always clear as to when s. 25 applies; for example, in *Newtons of Wembley Ltd* v. *Williams* [1964] 3 All ER 532 it was decided that a buyer in possession who resold goods would have to act in accordance with the requirements of a mercantile agent. Also, if the seller of the goods did not have good title, then the buyer in possession having purchased such goods from that seller, cannot pass good title under s. 25.

Sale of motor vehicles on hire purchase

Ownership of motor vehicles purchased on hire purchase remains with the seller until all instalments have been paid and the option to purchase exercised. Should a buyer sell a car subject to a hire purchase agreement to a third party, then the car can be recovered. However, the Hire Purchase Act 1964, Part III provides an exception to a private person who buys a motor vehicle subject to a hire purchase agreement in good faith without notice of defect in title. Because he has bought in good faith, he can then pass on good title to another private person. Any motor dealer or finance company who buys such a vehicle is not protected as they are not seen as private purchasers and are in a position to check a register of hire purchase agreements.

Market overt

This applies to goods sold before 3 January 1994 in an established market, in the normal market usage between the hours of sunrise and sunset, to a buyer who acted in good faith without knowledge of defect of title. Section 22 SGA 1979, which allowed this exception, was repealed by the SG(A)A 1994 because it effectively allowed a thief to pass good title.

■ Putting it all together

Answer guidelines

See the essay question at the start of the chapter.

Approaching the question

Structure your answer so that you explain the rules on transfer of ownership and reservation of title, before addressing the alternative scenarios. Distinguish clearly between the law regarding unmixed and mixed goods before proceeding to examine how the courts have dealt with individual claims for goods manufactured out of the goods sold.

Important points to include

- Give a brief summary of the passing of ownership for specific and unascertained goods.
- Define a reservation of title clause.
- Explain the purpose of these clauses.
- Outline the rules on passing of ownership on insolvency of the buyer.
- Explain the effect of a reservation of title clause in cases of unmixed and mixed goods.
- Analyse and comment upon the decisions in cases involving mixed goods.

 Make your answer stand out

Point out the lack of clarity in the law regarding reservation of title clauses. Highlight the impracticality of trying to separate the identity of goods from a finished product where the goods have been mixed. Use cases such as *Re Peachdart* to illustrate how the courts have tried to resolve this by construing a reservation of title clause as establishing a 'charge' on property that will only be enforceable if registered.

READ TO IMPRESS

Webb, D. (2000) Title and Transformation: Who Owns Manufactured Goods? *Journal of Business Law* 513

Willett, C., Morgan-Taylor, M. and Naidoo, A. (2004) The Sale and Supply of Goods to Consumers Regulations, *Journal of Business Law* 94

www.pearsoned.co.uk/lawexpress

Go online to access more revision support including quizzes to test your knowledge, sample questions with answer guidelines, podcasts you can download, and more!

Sale and supply of goods 3:

Performance and remedies

5

Revision checklist

Essential points you should know:

☐ Duties of the seller regarding delivery of goods
☐ The rules on acceptance by the buyer
☐ The duty to pay the price
☐ Specific remedies for the seller and buyer

■ Topic map

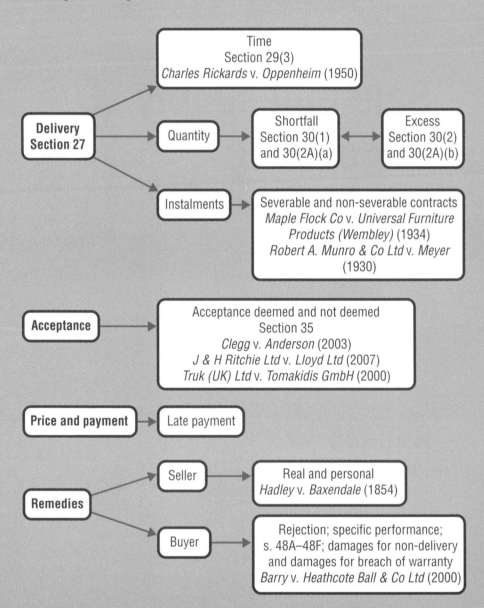

■ Introduction

Where parties to a contract for sale of goods do not make adequate provision in their agreements for delivery, acceptance or remedies, then the Sale of Goods Act 1979 will apply.

ASSESSMENT ADVICE

Essay questions

These could focus on one aspect of performance, and would expect you to demonstrate detailed knowledge of the rules and their effects.

Problem questions

These may cover *performance* by focusing on scenarios that cover all aspects of performance, or where one or both parties fail to perform a single performance obligation. In both essay and problem questions you will need to address remedies.

■ Sample question

Could you answer this question? Below is a typical problem question that could arise on this topic. Guidelines on answering the question are included at the end of this chapter, whilst a sample essay question and guidance on tackling it can be found on the companion website.

PROBLEM QUESTION

Eve has been running a garden centre for the past 20 years. She regularly deals with Heavenly Gardens Ltd (HG) for the purchase of garden supplies. Sometimes orders are delivered in instalments and at other times as an entire contract.

Lately HG has failed to deliver the right type and quantity of plants. On occasions deliveries have been late. When deliveries of garden tools are made to Eve, she tends not to check them until they are ready to be sold. Sometimes she has found that some of the tools are defective or of the wrong specification.

HG has caused much inconvenience to Eve who is beginning to fear a loss of reputation because of poor quality products and service provided to customers. Furthermore, Eve ▶

has suffered a substantial financial loss owing to a failure to honour several contracts for the supply of plants for garden parties and public events.

Advise Eve as to:

(a) HG's liability for poor performance of the contract.
(b) The remedies available to her should she succeed in a claim for breach of contract.

■ Delivery, acceptance and payment

KEY STATUTE

Sale of Goods Act 1979, s. 27

It is the duty of the seller to deliver the goods and the duty of the buyer to accept them, and pay the price.

Delivery

Delivery means transfer of possession, but not necessarily ownership, and may consist of:

- Delivering goods to a carrier for transport to the buyer.
- Delivering documents of title, such as bills of lading.
- Delivering the means of control of the goods to the buyer, for example, the keys to a car.
- Giving goods to a third party who acknowledges holding them on behalf of the buyer.

Unless otherwise agreed, delivery by the seller gives right to payment (s. 28 SGA 1979). Because the seller's duty to deliver and the buyer's duty to pay are concurrent, the seller can retain the goods until they are paid for.

Time of delivery

Delivery times are often fixed in the contract of sale and if a specified time is not adhered to the buyer has the right to terminate the contract for non-delivery. Sometimes a buyer waives their right to treat the contract as breached for non-delivery by accepting a much later delivery date. A buyer can still revive this right by giving reasonable notice of an intention to repudiate for non-delivery.

KEY CASE

Charles Rickards v. *Oppenheim* **[1950] 1 All ER 420**

Concerning: giving reasonable notice of right to repudiate for breach of a condition

Facts

A *term* in a contract for the supply of a specialist car, to be delivered within seven months, stated that time was of the essence. Despite the fact that the car was not delivered in the specified time, the defendant waived his 'right to repudiate' by agreeing to wait longer. After 10 months, however, the defendant gave notice of his intention to repudiate the contract if the car was not ready within a further month's time. Some 15 weeks later the claimants told the defendant that the car was now ready for delivery.

Legal principle

Having revived his right to repudiate the contract for breach of a *condition*, the defendant had every reason to refuse delivery of the car at the much later date.

Where no fixed time has been agreed, delivery must be within a *reasonable* time according to s. 29(3) and what is reasonable will depend upon the circumstances in each case. It is the duty of the buyer to accept delivery once the goods are ready, otherwise, any delay by the buyer to take delivery (at the seller's request) entitles the seller, under s. 37, to make a reasonable charge for care and custody of the goods.

Delivery of wrong quantity

As for a seller who delivers a shortfall or excess in the quantity of goods ordered, then s. 30 SGA 1979 applies. An amendment was introduced by SSGA 1994 to stop commercial buyers from abusing their right of rejection on unreasonable grounds. By contrast, the rights of consumer buyers are not affected by this amendment.

Delivery of a shortfall under s. 30(1) and s. 30(2A)(a)	Delivery of a greater quantity under s. 30(2) and s. 30(2A)(b)
Buyer may reject the whole consignment	Buyer may reject the whole consignment
Buyer may accept but will have to pay for the goods at the contract rate	Buyer may accept the goods contracted for but reject the rest
Trivial deviations (s. 30(2A)(a))	**Trivial deviations (s. 30(2A)(b))**
Commercial buyers cannot reject the whole consignment if it would be unreasonable to do so	Commercial buyers cannot reject the whole consignment if it would be unreasonable to do so

A right of partial rejection

In some cases a seller delivers a consignment made up of a mixture of contracted and non-contracted goods. Also, some of the goods in a consignment may be defective. And if that were the case, a right of partial rejection is granted by s. 35A SGA 1979 enabling the buyer to:

- Accept all conforming and reject all non-conforming goods.
- Accept all conforming goods and reject some of the non-conforming goods.
- Reject all the goods.
- Keep all the goods.
- Keep most of the goods, but reject only the seriously defective goods.

Delivery by instalments

Goods in commercial contracts are frequently delivered by way of instalments. Whether or not a **contract is severable** is a crucial factor in ascertaining a buyer's right of rejection for unsatisfactory instalments.

KEY DEFINITION: Severable contract

This term refers to a contract that can be divided individually with each part being treated separately.

Section 31 of SGA 1979 provides for three situations where disputes can arise owing to delivery by instalments.

Nature of agreement in delivery by instalments	Remedy for the buyer
1. No agreement as to delivery by instalments	Section 31(1): the buyer is not bound to accept delivery by instalments. If he does accept them, he must pay for them but he is entitled to refuse later deliveries.
2. There is agreement to deliver by instalments and the contract is not severable	Breach of a condition in the first instalment will entitle the buyer to repudiate the whole contract. But if one or more instalments have been accepted, he will not be able to reject later instalments if there is a breach of a condition regarding them.

Nature of agreement in delivery by instalments	Remedy for the buyer
3. There is an agreement to deliver by instalments and the contract is severable	If one or more instalments have been accepted, later instalments can be rejected if there is a breach of a condition (s. 31(2)).

✎ EXAM TIP

Candidates can make the mistake of assuming that where an instalment is paid for separately, it is naturally a severable contract that gives a person the right to repudiate the entire contract. This is not necessarily the case, as s. 31(2) makes clear when it distinguishes between severable breaches; some of which may give rise to rights to repudiate the entire contract, and others, the right to compensation only.

! Don't be tempted to...

Be sure not to overlook repudiation of whole or part of the contract in severable agreements. Suppose that a contract is severable, when can the buyer regard the whole contract as repudiated? When applying s. 31(2) the court will first assess the degree of seriousness of the breach and will then look at the likelihood of the breach being repeated. The buyer's rights of rejection will depend on the facts in each case, as the following decisions demonstrate.

KEY CASE

Maple Flock Co. v. *Universal Furniture Products (Wembley)* **[1934] 1 KB 148**
Concerning: application of s. 31(2) to severable agreements

Facts
The first 15 instalments in a contract to supply 100 tons of flock were satisfactory, as were instalments 17, 18, 19 and 20. Because instalment 16 was proven to be defective, the buyers claimed the right to repudiate the whole contract.

Legal principle
As to whether the buyer was entitled to repudiate the contract depended upon two factors. On the one hand, what was the degree of the breach, and on the other, what ▶

was the likelihood of it recurring? On neither of these grounds could the court hold the breach to be serious enough to warrant repudiation. Even if there had been a clause stating that each instalment was to be a separate contract, the courts would still regard this as *one* contract, which happened to be severable.

KEY CASE

Robert A. Munro & Co Ltd v. *Meyer* [1930] 2 KB 312

Concerning: the buyer's right to repudiate the whole contract

Facts

This case concerned a contract for the sale of 1,500 tons of bone and meal by instalments. As the first instalment, representing 651 tons, was adulterated, the buyers wished to repudiate the entire contract.

Legal principle

There was no obligation on the part of the buyer to accept any future instalments owing to the extent of their current loss.

Acceptance by the buyer

Whilst, at common law, the general rule is that an acceptance completes a legal agreement and therefore cannot be revoked, the Sale of Goods Act 1979 does recognise that in certain situations, although on the face of it acceptance appears to have taken place, its completion can be delayed. Section 34 SGA 1979 gives the right for the buyer to examine the goods at delivery and, if the sale is by sample, to compare the bulk of the goods with the sample. Provisions governing acceptance are contained in s. 35, which was significantly amended by the Sale and Supply of Goods Act 1994, and the Sale and Supply of Goods to Consumers Regulations 2002. The amendment to s. 35 states that the buyer is *deemed to have accepted* the goods in the following situations.

When a buyer is deemed to have accepted goods

Relevant section in Sale of Goods Act 1979	Three circumstances in which the buyer is deemed to have accepted goods
Section 35(1)(a) and (b)	1. When he intimates to the seller that he has accepted them.

Relevant section in Sale of Goods Act 1979	Three circumstances in which the buyer is deemed to have accepted goods
	2. When the goods have been delivered to him and he does any act ... inconsistent with the ownership of the seller.
Section 35(4)	3. When after the lapse of a reasonable time he retains the goods without intimating to the seller that he has rejected them.

Yet, as the section goes on to state, under s. 35(2) and (5) the buyer is not deemed to have accepted unexamined delivered goods until he has had a reasonable opportunity to examine them and, furthermore, when the buyer is a consumer, they cannot be asked to sign away these rights (s. 35(3)).

KEY CASE

Clegg v. *Andersson* [2003] 2 Lloyd's Rep 32 (CA)

Concerning: non-acceptance of goods under s. 35(1)(a)(b) and s. 35(4)

Facts

Clegg entered into a contract for the purchase of a yacht from Andersson for £236,000 in November 1999. The yacht was delivered to Clegg on 12 August 2000 at which time Andersson told Clegg that the keel was much heavier than the weight given in the manufacturer's specification. Despite this, Clegg told Andersson that he liked the way the yacht handled, having taken it on an eight-day cruise. Later, however, Clegg told Andersson that he did not like the extra stability that the weight gave to the yacht and Andersson told Clegg he would reduce the weight of the keel. Clegg asked for a delay whilst he consulted his advisers and then eventually rejected the yacht on 6 March 2001. The trial judge held that there had been no breach of s. 14(2) and that Clegg had lost his right of rejection under s. 35.

Legal principle

The Court of Appeal held that the yacht was not of satisfactory quality and that Clegg had not intimated his acceptance under s. 35(1)(a): leaving his personal possessions on the yacht did not intimate acceptance, nor did his initial statement that he liked the way the yacht sailed, as his later reservations indicated otherwise. Neither had Clegg accepted under s. 35(1)(b) because he had done nothing inconsistent with the ownership of the seller. Finally, Clegg had not accepted the yacht under s. 35(4) by keeping it longer than reasonable, because according to s. 59, what is a reasonable ▶

time is a question of fact. As Clegg had not received all the information he needed to decide on repair until three weeks before he decided to reject the yacht, agreement to have the drill inspected and if necessary repaired, did not allow an informed decision about whether or not to reject the goods.

When a buyer is not deemed to have accepted goods

The 1994 amendment to s. 35 added two more provisions to protect a buyer's right of rejection.

Relevant provision in Sale of Goods Act 1979	Circumstances in which a buyer is not deemed to have accepted goods
Section 35(6)	(a) when he asks for or agrees to their repair by or under an arrangement with the seller, or (b) where the goods are delivered to another under a sub-sale or other disposition

KEY CASE

J & H Ritchie Ltd v. Lloyd Ltd [2007] 1 WLR 670

Concerning: the right to reject goods after a repair

Fact

A farmer bought a seed drill and set of harrows. On first use, the drill was found to be faulty and he returned it to the seller for inspection and possible repair. After a few weeks, the seller told the farmer that the drill had been fixed and was ready for collection. When the farmer asked about what was wrong with the drill, the seller would only proffer that it was 'repaired to factory-gate specification'. As it stood, the farmer was dissatisfied with this response because he could not test the drill and harrows until the next season. Uncertain of its reliability, he sought to reject it and reclaim the purchase price.

Legal principle

Agreement to have the drill inspected and if necessary repaired, did not constitute *acceptance* by the farmer. He needed to know the nature of the fault in order to make an informed decision about whether or not to reject the goods. Under the circumstances he was entitled to repudiate the agreement and recover the purchase price.

Truk (UK) Ltd v. *Tomakidis GmbH* [2000] 1 Lloyd's Rep 543

Concerning: what constitutes a reasonable time for rejection of goods intended for sub-sale

Facts

Tomakidis, the buyer, made a contract with Truk, the seller, to supply and fit an under-lift to a lorry chassis. Truk was aware that Tomakidis intended to sell the lorry to a sub-buyer. Tomakidis was told by the potential sub-buyer that the under-lift was unsuitable, and after official confirmation of its unsuitability for purpose, Tomakidis sought to reject it, some nine months after purchase.

Legal principle

Where goods are sold for re-sale, a reasonable time for rejection should be the time taken to re-sell, plus extra time for the sub-buyer to test out the goods. In this case, a reasonable amount of time is the first six months when the buyer first questioned suitability of the product, plus another three months for investigation of the suitability of the product. So, Tomakidis was entitled to reject the goods after nine months because he had not, in fact, ever accepted them.

✓ Make your answer stand out

All buyers, particularly consumers, are now in a stronger position when they wish to reject defective or unsuitable goods. A consumer's signature on a delivery note is now meaningless in the absence of any opportunity to examine the goods. Also, even where goods have been examined prior to purchase, a consumer has the right to request a further opportunity to examine them. As regards business buyers, s. 35 can be excluded by agreement, subject to the test of reasonableness in UCTA 1977, whereas s. 35A gives the buyer the right of partial rejection in that they can accept some of the goods and reject others, as long as they do not form part of a commercial unit (s. 35(7)).

! Don't be tempted to…

Do not overlook the protection to consumers offered by the Cancellation of Contracts made in a Consumer's Home or Place of Work Regulations 2008. These regulations grant a cooling-off period of seven days to any consumer who has entered into a contract as a result of 'doorstep' selling.

Price and payment

It is a legal duty of the buyer to pay the contract price at the time of delivery unless any other contractual agreement has been made to the contrary. How the price is fixed is covered by s. 8 SGA 1979.

□ REVISION NOTE

Details on s. 8 SGA 1979 are given in Chapter 3 as an aspect of consideration. Basically, s. 8 states that the price or how it is to be agreed may be fixed by contract, or may even be determined by a course of dealing. Where no provision for price is made within a contract, the buyer must pay a 'reasonable price' depending on factors like the quality of the goods and their intended use.

Late payment of price will constitute a breach of warranty under SGA 1979, unless the contract says otherwise (s. 10(1)).

Late Payment of Commercial Debts (Interest) Act 1998

Because small businesses suffer indebtedness due to late payment, the LPCD(I)A 1998 gives businesses the right to charge interest at 8% above the base rate without going to court. The interest is charged from the date on which it was agreed payment should be made. In the absence of any contractual payment date, the interest charge commences at 30 days after the contract has been performed, or, 30 days after the debtor has been given notice to pay. A court has the right to award this statutory rate of interest, should the business take legal action against the debtor.

! Don't be tempted to...

Don't forget to mention the practice of contracting out of the right to statutory interest. Commercial buyers in a dominant bargaining position may try to persuade small business sellers to forego their right to statutory interest by means of an exclusion clause within their contracts. Any term attempting to exclude a seller's right to claim statutory interest is declared void, unless a significant reward can be offered as an alternative remedy.

■ Remedies of the seller

The remedies that are available to a seller fall into two categories, **personal remedies** and **real remedies**.

KEY DEFINITION: Personal remedies

Remedies sought personally against the buyer for compensation of loss.

Unlike personal remedies, real remedies are aimed at the goods rather than the person.

KEY DEFINITION: Real remedies

Remedies sought against the goods themselves, in order that they may be retained by the seller.

Personal remedies of the seller

The following personal remedies are open to the seller:

- An action for the price.
- Damages for non-acceptance.
- Damages for refusal of delivery.
- Termination of the contract.

Action for the price under s. 49

An action for the price can be taken by a seller when the property has passed to the buyer (s. 49(1)) or when payment has not been made by a specified date, irrespective of whether the property in the goods has passed to the buyer (s. 49(2)). Both sections require that the buyer has wantonly neglected or refused to pay the price.

✎ EXAM TIP

It is worth pointing out that when suing for the price the rules of remoteness of damage as stated in *Hadley* v. *Baxendale* (see Key Case below) do not apply.

Damages for non-acceptance

An unpaid seller may prefer to sue for damages for non-acceptance in cases where a buyer neglects or refuses to accept and pay for the goods. The usual measure for damages is the loss directly resulting in the course of business from the buyer's breach (s. 50(2)). However, where there is an available market for the goods, s. 50(3) encourages the seller to claim the difference between the contract price and the market price at the time when the goods ought to have been accepted.

A problem arises when there is no available market for the goods in question. It could be that, owing to over-supply, there is no available market for the goods, so preventing the seller from mitigating any loss. If this was the case, the seller would be able to claim for actual loss as long as it was foreseeable within the rules of *Hadley* v. *Baxendale*. In this way, a seller could claim for loss of profits.

KEY CASE

Hadley v. *Baxendale* **(1854) 9 Exch 341**

Concerning: remoteness of damage

Facts

A miller sent his broken crankshaft for repair by means of the defendant carrier. The defendant was late in delivering the shaft and as a result, the mill was idle for a few days. On which grounds, the miller claimed damages for lost profits.

Legal principle

The court laid down the principles of remoteness of damage as follows:

(1) *Normal losses* as those that arise naturally from the breach (in the usual course of events) can be recovered.

(2) Damages for *abnormal losses* can only be recovered if the loss may reasonably be in the *contemplation* of the parties when they made the contract.

With regard to the above case, it was held that the losses outside rule 2 could not be claimed.

Damages for refusal of delivery

KEY STATUTE

Sale of Goods Act 1979, s. 37

When a seller, who is ready and willing to deliver goods, finds that a buyer does not take delivery within a reasonable time, then any loss caused by this delay (or charge for looking after and keeping the goods while awaiting take up) can be claimed against the buyer.

Clearly any damages claimed by the seller must compensate for delay in accepting delivery rather than for loss of a bargain that results from the delay. There again, reasonable charges for looking after the goods could include compensation for insurance or transport costs, too.

The seller's right to terminate the contract

Once the buyer repudiates a contract, the seller can 'accept' and with that treat the contract as terminated, and then claim for damages. Care should be taken when terminating a contract in this way in case the buyer takes an action against the seller for wrongful repudiation, as happened in the *Hong Kong Fir Shipping* case (see Chapter 2).

Real remedies of the seller

Real remedies are only available to an *unpaid* seller.

KEY STATUTE

Sale of Goods Act 1979, s. 38

A seller is unpaid:

(a) when the whole of the price has not been paid ...
(b) when a **bill of exchange** or other negotiable instrument has been received as conditional payment, and the condition ... has not been fulfilled

---

KEY DEFINITION: Bill of exchange

A negotiable instrument that is similar to a cheque. A person orders their bank to pay the bearer a fixed sum of money, but on a specific date.

The effect of s. 38 is to allow the seller to be defined as an unpaid seller where a buyer has been given credit or where the buyer pays by a cheque that is dishonoured.

In the face of a betrayal of payment, there are three real remedies available to an unpaid seller:

■ A **lien** on the goods.
■ The right to stop goods in transit.
■ The right to resell the goods.

Lien on the goods

KEY DEFINITION: Lien

The right to hold on to the property of another and keep it as security until an obligation has been performed.

An unpaid seller may exercise a lien over the goods even when ownership has passed to the buyer in the following circumstances:

- Where the goods have been sold without credit conditions.
- Where the goods have been sold on credit but the credit period has expired.
- Where the buyer has become insolvent.

As soon as the outstanding price has been paid by the buyer (or the buyer's liquidator), the seller will at once be obliged to hand over the goods. Nevertheless, the right to a lien is lost when the seller hands the goods to a carrier without retaining the right of disposal, or when the right to a lien has been given up. In a severable contract where each instalment is paid for separately, the seller cannot hold onto one instalment as a lien for another that has yet to be paid.

Stoppage in transit

Goods in transit can be stopped by the seller, before the goods are delivered to the buyer, only if the buyer has become insolvent (s. 46). When goods are sent to a destination that the buyer then alters, transit ceases, since the carrier is seen as retaining them on behalf of the buyer. So, goods cannot be stopped in transit should the buyer instruct a carrier to take them to another place. In practice, this right is rarely used in commercial cases as it is common for sellers to use retention of title clauses in their conditions of sale.

Right of resale

Section 48 provides a remedy for the right of 'resale of goods' in the following circumstances:

- Where the goods are perishable.
- Where the seller gives notice of his intention to resell and the buyer does not pay within a reasonable time.
- Where a term of the conditions of sale gives the unpaid seller the right of resale.

■ Buyer's remedies

Remedies available to the buyer include:

- The right of rejection.
- Specific performance.
- Remedies under ss. 48A–48F (consumer buyers only).
- Damages for non-delivery.
- Damages for breach of a warranty.

The right of rejection

Rights of rejection (or non-acceptance) have already been dealt with in analysing s. 35. As was said in Chapter 3, all types of buyers can repudiate a contract for breach of s. 12 SGA 1979. But whereas the right of rejection for breach of ss. 13–15 applies to consumers only, it may not apply to commercial buyers who reject goods for trivial reasons.

> 📖 **REVISION NOTE**
>
> Section 15A was referred to in Chapter 3 when discussing the decision in the *Re Moore and Landauer* case. This section limits the right of rejection for non-consumer buyers if the breach is so slight so as to make rejection seem unreasonable. Of course, a commercial buyer in negotiating terms of a sale can always insist that s. 15A does not apply, and will then retain full rights of rejection.

Specific performance

An order of specific performance requires the seller to fulfil an obligation to supply goods to a buyer but is rarely granted. It may be granted where a seller has agreed to sell a unique item, but will not be granted in the following situations:

- Where damages would be enough.
- To a party who has not behaved fairly.
- Against a party who would suffer undue hardship.
- In contracts involving personal services.
- In favour of or against a minor.

Remedies under ss. 48A–48F

For consumer buyers ss. 48A–48F provide remedies if the goods do not conform to the contract at any time from delivery for up to six months as follows:

- Replacement or repair of goods (s. 48A(2)(a) and s. 48B) subject to giving the seller reasonable time (s. 48D).
- Reduction of the price or rescission of the contract (s. 48A(2)(b)(i) and (ii) and s. 48C).
- An application by the consumer buyer for specific performance of the seller's obligation to repair or replace the goods (s. 48E(2)).
- Under s. 48E(4) a court can award another remedy under ss. 48B or 48C apart from that applied for. The court may also grant any ss. 48B or 48C remedy unconditionally or conditional as to damages, payment or as it sees fit.

It is important to note that the right to repair or replacement is not absolute and can be refused if it is impossible, or disproportionate to other remedies. Also, price reduction and **rescission** are available in circumstances where the seller has not replaced or repaired the goods within a reasonable time or where such replacement or repair would be to the buyer's inconvenience.

KEY DEFINITION: Rescission

Sets the contract aside and restores parties to pre-contractual position.

Damages for non-delivery

Provision for damages for non-delivery is effected by s. 51 SGA 1979.

KEY STATUTE

Sale of Goods Act 1979, s. 51

(1) Where the seller wrongfully neglects or refuses to deliver goods ... the buyer may maintain an action ... for damages for wrong delivery.
(2) The measure of damages is the estimated loss directly and naturally resulting, in the ordinary course of events, from the seller's breach of contract.
(3) Where there is an available market ... the measure of damages is *prima facie* ... the difference between the contract price and the market or the current price ... at the time they ought to have been delivered ...

This section allows a buyer to either mitigate their loss were the market price to have gone down, or fulfil their expectations of cost, should the market price have risen.

KEY CASE

Barry v. *Heathcote Ball & Co Ltd* [2000] 1 WLR 1962

Concerning: damages claimed by the buyer at the available market price

Facts

Barry bid £400 for two engine analysers at an auction. Given that the analysers were worth £14,000, the auctioneer refused to honour Barry's bid because he felt it was far too low. In fact, the analysers were sold at or around the market price to another buyer, a few days later. Barry sued for the difference between the market price and his bid, as no reserve price was set for the analysers at the auction.

> **Legal principle**
>
> In this case, the Court of Appeal inferred a collateral contract existed between the auctioneer and a potential buyer and in the absence of a reserve price the auctioneer should really have sold the analysers to Barry for £200 each. Because the auctioneer failed to honour this collateral obligation, Barry was entitled to claim the difference between the contract price and the market price.

As for profits from expected sub-sales, only foreseeable losses are recoverable.

Damages for breach of a warranty

Where there is a breach of a warranty, a buyer cannot reject the goods but can either sue the seller for damages, or deduct damages from the price of the goods under s. 53. The measure of damages is subject to the rule on recovery of normal losses under *Hadley* v. *Baxendale*. In a breach of a warranty of 'quality', the measure of damages will be the difference between the value of the defective goods and the value of the goods had they not been defective.

■ Putting it all together

Answer guidelines

See the problem question at the start of the chapter.

Approaching the question

The question is concerned with delivery, acceptance and rights of rejection in contracts that may be by instalments or entire, as well as remedies for the buyer.

Important points to include

- Time of delivery (s. 29).
- Quantity where there is a shortfall of delivered goods (s. 30(1); s. 30(2A)(a)) and where there is an excess: (s. 30(2); s. 30(2A)(b)). When the right of partial rejection operates (s. 35A).
- Right of rejection where the contract is by instalments and the contract is severable (s. 31).
- Acceptance of the tools (s. 35(3)).

▶

■ Remedies of the buyer: rejection subject to triviality (s. 15A); damages for non-delivery (s. 51); damages for breach of warranty (subject to the rule of remoteness of damage).

 Make your answer stand out

Focus on the facts given in the problem in order to apply relevant sections of SGA 1979. Also, you need to identify Eve as a commercial rather than a consumer buyer. With regard to late delivery, you should mention that in the absence of contrary agreement, s. 29(3) SGA 1979 states that delivery should be within a reasonable time and what is reasonable depends on the circumstances. When addressing the delivery of incorrect quantities of plants you will need to detail Eve's rights of rejection, pointing out that the s. 30(2A)(a) and (b) provisions for trivial deviations apply to commercial buyers (but not consumer buyers). As regards the tools, show that you understand the right of partial rejection granted by s. 35A for defective goods. Where delivery of any of the goods is by instalments, you need to emphasise that whether the contract is severable or not will determine Eve's right of rejection. Don't forget to give detail of Eve's remedies under s. 31. Use case law to demonstrate whether or not Eve can reject the entire contract. When looking at deemed acceptance, you need to bear in mind that the facts of the problem limit your considerations to s. 35(4). Finally, when explaining remedies you should point out that damages for non-delivery under s. 51 are for consequential loss, whereas damages for breach of warranty are subject to the remoteness of damage rules.

READ TO IMPRESS

Adams, J. N. (2002) Damages in Sale of Goods: A Critique of the Provisions of the Sale of Goods Act and Article 2 on the Uniform Commercial Code, *Journal of Business Law* 553

Dobson, P. (2003) Sale of Goods – Loss of Right of Rejection – Acceptance, *Student Law Review* 40

Low, K. F. K. (2007) Repair, Rejection and Rescission: An Uneasy Resolution, 123 *Law Quarterly Review* 536

Willett, C., Morgan-Taylor, M. and Naidoo, A. N. (2004) The Sale and Supply of Goods to Consumers Regulations, *Journal of Business Law* 94

www.pearsoned.co.uk/lawexpress

 Go online to access more revision support including quizzes to test your knowledge, sample questions with answer guidelines, podcasts you can download, and more!

Distance selling and electronic commerce

6

Revision checklist

Essential points you should know:

- [ ] The scope of the Consumer Protection (Distance Selling) Regulations 2000
- [ ] How a contract is processed online
- [ ] Key provisions of regulations regarding electronic communications and signatures
- [ ] The implications of making international contracts online

■ Topic map

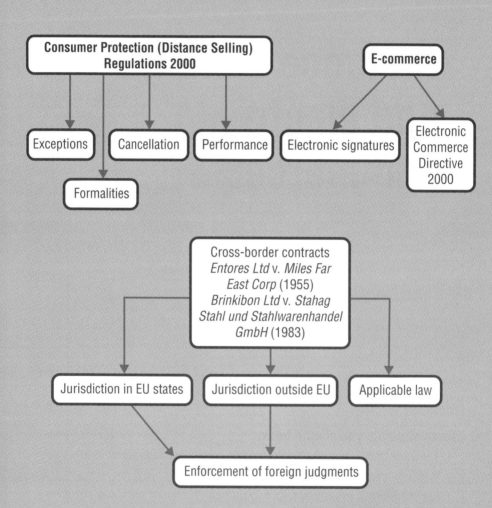

■ Introduction

Exam questions increasingly call for an analysis of distance contracts, usually conducted over the internet.

You will have already encountered the problems caused by instantaneous communication in the formation of contracts, most notably those of choice of jurisdiction in international transactions. Special rules for withdrawal from contracts have also been addressed in the context of distance selling agreements. Because both distance selling and electronic contracts are concerned with a mode of contracting, you should be aware of the relevant applicable common law and regulatory regime. This chapter focuses on the key common law and statutory provisions that apply to distance and online selling.

ASSESSMENT ADVICE

Essay questions

These tend to include a general statement which may or may not involve online trading. If the question is concerned with online sales, you should deal with distance selling as well as e-commerce. You will need to demonstrate a sound knowledge of the provisions of all relevant regulations.

Problem questions

Problems tend to take the form of a scenario in which a customer enters into a distance contract, either online or by other means of communication. You will need to be aware of the subject matter of the deal to ensure that the Consumer Protection (Distance Selling) Regulations 2000 do apply. Also look out for possible face-to-face contact between customer and seller during the transaction. If the transaction involves cross-border issues, you will be required to demonstrate knowledge of the Brussels Regulation and the Contracts (Applicable Law) Act 1990.

■ Sample question

Could you answer this question? Below is a typical essay question that could arise on this topic. Guidelines on answering the question are included at the end of this chapter, whilst a sample problem question and guidance on tackling it can be found on the companion website.

■ Distance selling

The aim of the Distance Selling Directive 97/7/EC is to give consumers who make contracts without any face-to-face contact with the supplier, protection throughout the EU. In order to achieve consumer protection, the Directive addresses issues such as the provision of adequate pre-contractual information, cancellation rights, inertia selling and fraudulent use of credit cards. The Directive has been implemented into UK law by the Consumer Protection (Distance Selling) Regulations 2000.

□ REVISION NOTE

It is important to be aware that inertia selling, when goods or services are supplied without the offeree's agreement, is considered an offence under the Unsolicited Goods and Services Act 1971 (s. 2) and an automatically unfair trade practice under the Consumer Protection from Unfair Trading Regulations 2008 (Sch. 1) (see Chapter 11).

KEY STATUTE

Unsolicited Goods and Services Act 1971, s. 2

Section 2 states that any trade or business person who, without reasonable cause to believe he has a right to payment, demands payment for **unsolicited goods** sent to another person, shall be guilty of a summary offence and if found guilty can be fined up to £200.

KEY DEFINITION: Unsolicited goods

Unrequested goods sent to the *offeree* without their consent.

Consumer Protection (Distance Selling) Regulations 2000

These somewhat complex Regulations insist that, for those contracts affected by the Regulations, clear detailed information about the product and supplier must be provided prior to the contract. This enables the consumer-buyer to be well informed before they decide to make an offer. And because the Regulations do not state the point at which the contract is entered into – as this is for the common law and the parties' own terms to determine – many of these contracts are easily cancellable. It goes without saying that these sorts of agreements have a cooling-off period, during which a consumer can withdraw from the contract.

KEY DEFINITION: Distance contract

Under reg. 3(1) a 'distance contract' is one which is between a supplier acting for commercial or professional purposes and a *consumer* who is a natural person acting for purposes outside his business. It must concern goods or services and be conducted under an *organised distance sales or service scheme* run by the supplier. Finally, the supplier must make exclusive use of distance communications such as telephone, fax, television, letter, email, internet, up to and at the time the contract is made.

✎ EXAM TIP

Look out for problem questions in which there is a series of distance communications in contract negotiations, but where the contract is made face-to-face. This will not qualify as 'distance selling', neither will a one-off telephone or online order made by a customer. Also, it is important to understand that the term 'organised sales or service scheme' refers to a bespoke scheme for distance selling, such as an established home delivery service, rather than a one-off event.

Excepted contracts

Contracts may fall within the definition given in reg. 3, but if they are 'excepted contracts' according to reg. 5, they will not be categorised as 'distance contracts'. So none of the provisions of the Regulations apply. Excepted contracts include:

- The sale or disposition of an interest in land (excluding rental).
- The construction of a building where the sale of an interest in land is included.
- The provision of financial services.
- With automated vending machines or on automated commercial premises.
- Concluded by payphone with a telecommunications operator.
- Auction sales.

Other exemptions

The requirements for prior information and cancellation provisions only, do not apply to the following contracts:

- The supply of food or drink to a consumer's residence or workplace by a regular rounds person (reg. 6(2)(a)).

- Accommodation, transport, catering or leisure services contracted for a specific date or period (reg. 6(2)(b)).
- Timeshare agreements (regs. 7–20) and package tours (regs. 7–19(1)).

Formalities required for distance contracts

The Regulations aim to ensure that consumers are given appropriate information and offered cancellation rights when making distance contracts during pre-contractual negotiations, before and during contractual performance. If any of these requirements are not followed, the contract is unenforceable.

Information requirements

Stage of contractual formation	Information required to be given to consumer
Pre-contract (reg. 7)	Supplier's identity and address if any advance payment is given
	Description of goods/services
	Price (inclusive of taxes), delivery costs and any costs of using distance communication
	The duration of any offer or price
	The minimum duration of an ongoing or recurrent contract
	Arrangements for payment, delivery and performance
	The existence of rights of cancellation
Pre-contract, before or during performance (reg. 8)	Supplier's geographical business address for complaints as well as name, code or reference number
	After-sales service or guarantees
	Cancellation rights and methods including contracts of unspecified duration or exceeding one year

Any information provided must be clear, comprehensible and appropriate with regard to the method of distance communication and given in a spirit of good faith by the supplier.

Furthermore, information required by reg. 8 should be given to the consumer in durable form in good time either before or during the contract's performance.

 Make your answer stand out

On the face of it, reg. 7 of the Consumer Protection (Distance Selling) Regulations 2000 appears to be an effective provision as it insists that information about the price and any surcharges a company makes must be given to the consumer before a contract is concluded. Yet, travel companies have effectively hidden credit card surcharges by only making consumers aware of them just before the contract is finalised, and only then after negotiating several web pages of form-filling and box ticking. So now the OFT has advised that surcharges be made clear earlier on in the transaction, or better still, be included in the service price. However, the OFT cannot implement these recommendations until they have been directed to do so by the EU.

Cancellation provisions

Any consumer who wishes to exercise rights of cancellation must send written notice to the supplier within the cancellation period.

Nature of transaction	Expiry of period of notice for cancellation
Sale of goods	Seven working days after delivery
Supply of services	Seven working days after the contract is made
Sale of goods or supply of service where supplier has failed to give certain information in durable medium	The earlier of the following: (a) Seven working days after supplier complies with requirement, or (b) Three months and seven working days after delivery of the goods or making the contract for services Hence, if the supplier *never* complies with the requirement to give information in a durable form, (b) applies

Once a consumer has exercised a right to cancel, payments made or goods given in part exchange can be recovered and the consumer must return goods to the supplier. Should the consumer's credit, debit, or charge card be used fraudulently to pay for a distance contract, then that payment can be cancelled by the consumer.

Contract performance

Once a distance contract has been made, the Regulations provide the following default rules for performance of the contract:

- The supplier should carry out the contract within a maximum time period of 30 days starting with the day after the consumer submitted an order.

- The supplier must give notice of his inability to perform and repay the consumer within 30 days of giving notice.

- If an outdoor event cannot be rescheduled, no refund need be given if the parties agree.

- The supplier may offer an alternative performance if unable to perform as agreed on condition that the consumer has clear prior knowledge of this arrangement, it was provided for in the contract and any costs of returning goods that are cancelled are borne by the supplier.

■ E-commerce

The following legislation applies to electronic contracts:

- Electronic Communications Act 2000.
- Electronic Signatures Regulations 2002.
- Electronic Commerce (EC Directive) Regulations 2002.

Electronic signatures

The Electronic Signatures Directive 1999/93/EC was implemented into the UK by the Electronic Communications Act 2000 and the Electronic Signatures Regulations 2002.

Electronic Communications Act 2000	Electronic Signatures Regulations 2002
Provides for the legal recognition of electronic signatures	Introduces a statutory approved scheme to act as a quality mark for providers of cryptography services
Electronic signatures are admissible as evidence of authenticity and integrity (s. 7)	
Government ministers have the power to amend any legislation to authorise or facilitate the use of electronic communications and storage (s. 8)	

Electronic Commerce Directive 2000

The Electronic Commerce Directive 2000 was implemented into the UK by the Electronic Commerce (EC Directive) Regulations 2002 which applies to all **service providers**.

KEY DEFINITION: Service provider

A broad definition is given by reg. 2(1) to include:

'... any service normally provided for remuneration at a distance by means of electronic equipment for the processing (including digital compression) and storage of data, and at the individual request of a recipient of a service.'

! Don't be tempted to...

Don't assume that a service provider refers solely to the server. In fact, according to reg. 2(1), a service provider includes those who advertise or sell goods and services to customers (both business and consumers) online, as well as those who transmit or store electronic data or provide access to a communications network.

Information to be provided

Whilst businesses who deal with each other can make their own arrangements about the provision of information, a business dealing with consumers must follow the requirements laid down by the Regulations. Hence, the service provider must give their name and geographical address as well as direct contact details. If the service provider belongs to an authorisation scheme, the customer must be directed to relevant codes of conduct that can be accessed electronically. Finally, details of a trade or other register and registration ID must be provided if relevant. The service provider must also provide the technical steps to follow to conclude the contract and state whether or not the final contract will be filed by the business and whether it will be accessible to the customer. If the service provider fails to comply with these requirements then the customer can claim damages under reg. 13.

Placing of an order

Where an order is placed, the service provider must:

- Acknowledge receipt of the order quickly and electronically.

- Provide the technical means to identify and correct input errors before finalising the order so that the customer can cancel.

- The customer should also be provided with the languages offered for conclusion of the contract.

If terms and conditions apply, the service provider must make them available for storage or printing out.

Of course, if a contract is formed and concluded solely by email, the above requirements do not apply.

Cross-border contracts

When a contract is made between parties in different countries issues of jurisdiction, applicable law and enforcement of judgments arise.

Jurisdiction in EU states

Choice of jurisdiction in the EU is governed by the Brussels Regulation (Council Regulation 44/2001). Usually, jurisdiction for contract lies with the country of the defendant's domicile. A natural person's domicile is the country where he lives or to which he is substantially connected. A company's domicile is where it was incorporated and has its registered office or some other branch, or where its central control and management is exercised. There are, of course, exceptions to this general rule.

Exceptions concerning cross-border contracts

Branch or agency	Consumer claims (Art. 15)	Country of performance
If a defendant company has a branch in the EU, it can be sued at that branch, even if the main company is in another state within the EU or even outside the EU	(a) A consumer who buys goods or services from a supplier in another EU state, can sue in the consumer's own state	A claim in contract can be brought either in the country where the defendant is domiciled or in the country where the contract was due to be performed

Branch or agency	Consumer claims (Art. 15)	Country of performance
	(b) A consumer who buys goods from a website in another Member State, may sue in his own country providing the website is available in the consumer's domicile	
	(c) A consumer who buys in response to an advertisement in another Member State, can sue in his own country if that advertisement is also directed to his country	

Jurisdiction where one of the parties is outside the EU

Where either the buyer or seller is domiciled outside the EU the Brussels Regulation will not apply. In such cases the English courts will only accept jurisdiction if:

- The contract was made in England.
- The contract was made by an agent based in England on behalf of a party trading or living elsewhere.
- The relevant applicable law is English.
- The contract specified the High Court as choice of forum.

KEY CASE

Entores Ltd v. *Miles Far East Corp* [1955] 2 QB 327

Concerning: communication of acceptances by electronic means

Facts

The claimants were based in London and the defendants in the Netherlands. An acceptance of the claimants' counter offer was sent by telex machine from the Netherlands. The English company had to establish where the contract was formed. ▶

Legal principle

The contract was formed in England, so the English court had jurisdiction. The rule concerning acceptances sent by instantaneous means is that the acceptance must arrive for it to be effective.

In *Brinkibon Ltd* v. *Stahag und Stahlwarenhandel GmbH* [1983] 2 AC 34 the House of Lords approved the above decision, extending the principle to all communication sent by electronic means.

KEY CASE

Brinkibon Ltd v. *Stahag und Stahlwarenhandel GmbH* **[1983] 2 AC 34**

Concerning: country of jurisdiction for the purpose of electronic communication

Facts

An English company wanted leave to sue an Austrian company for breach of contract. The question before the court was whether the contract had been made in London or Vienna. The acceptance of a counter offer had been telexed from London to Vienna.

Legal principle

The contract was formed in Vienna, so the English court did not have jurisdiction. (Note: This case would now be governed by the Brussels Convention.)

Applicable law

The Rome Convention, implemented into the UK by the Law of Contracts (Applicable Law) Act 1990, specifies that the law that applies to a contract is that chosen by the parties. The applicable law does not have to be the law of the country of jurisdiction. Where parties have failed to make a choice of law, then the applicable law will be the law of the country that has the closest connection to the contract. Usually, this will be the law of the country of the party who has to perform the contract. This means that the applicable law, in the absence of choice, will be that of the seller. The 1990 Act applies to contracts made before 17 December 2009. Contracts made after 17 December 2009 are governed by the new Rome 1 Regulation (EC) No. 593/2008, which harmonises the rules for contractual obligations.

 Make your answer stand out

Parties may try to choose a law to avoid the strict regulatory requirements of a country. This is pointless, because if litigation is conducted in a country with mandatory legislation but with a different applicable law, the mandatory provisions will apply.

Hence, any case brought in England using a foreign applicable law could not avoid the provisions of the Unfair Contract Terms Act 1977, the Unfair Terms in Consumer Contracts Regulations 1999 or the Consumer Protection (Distance Selling) Regulations 2000. For an interesting account of a cross-border judgment where an English mandatory provision was applied to Belgian applicable law using injunctive powers provided by Part 8 of the Enterprise Act 2002, see *Fair Trading*, Issue 43, March 2006, OFT.

Enforcement of a foreign judgment

Article 26 of the Brussels Convention provides that a judgment given in a contracting state shall be recognised in the other contracting states without any special procedure being required. The English court need not enquire into the jurisdiction of the EU court; it must assume it had jurisdiction and enforce its judgment, although there is a right of appeal. The procedure is by simple registration and application to the High Court. As regards non-European judgments, these are subject to common law rules and enquiries by the English court into foreign jurisdiction.

■ Putting it all together

Answer guidelines

See the essay question at the start of the chapter.

Approaching the question

You should initially define an online contract as a distance contract which is subject to the Consumer Protection (Distance Selling) Regulations 2000 as well as the Electronic Commerce (EC Directive) Regulations 2002.

Important points to include

Deal with each Regulation by analysing key definitions such as 'distance sale' and 'service provider'.

You need to point out that the Consumer Protection (Distance Selling) Regulations 2000 apply to consumers only and the Electronic Commerce (EC Directive) Regulations 2002 apply to both businesses and consumers. ▶

Give an outline of the protective measures given to customers (consumers and/ or businesses) including information requirements, rights of cancellation, rules for contractual performance and online procedures.

Because of the development of international markets via the internet, you should include choice of jurisdiction, applicable law and enforcement of judgments.

When dealing with the above issues you will need to apply key provisions of the relevant Regulations.

 ## Make your answer stand out

The question requires an assessment of the degree of protection offered to those entering into distance contracts, so you should include areas where protection is lacking, for example the exceptions and exemptions in distance selling. Additionally you should point out that whilst the E-Commerce (EC Directive) Regulations do not apply to contracts conducted by email, such contracts, if business to consumer, would be subject to the CP(DS) Regulations. With regard to cross-border contracts, highlight the greater protection given to EU members trading within the EU and highlight the special protection offered to consumers by the Brussels Regulation, Art. 15.

READ TO IMPRESS

Meads, P. (2002) E-consumer Protection – Distance Selling, *International Company and Commercial Law Review* 179

Youngerwood, A. and Mann, S. (2000) Extra Armoury for Consumers. The New Distance Selling Regulations, *Journal of Information Law & Technology* (3)

 www.pearsoned.co.uk/lawexpress

Go online to access more revision support including quizzes to test your knowledge, sample questions with answer guidelines, podcasts you can download, and more!

Product liability

7

Revision checklist

Essential points you should know:

- [ ] Consumer protection under contract
- [ ] Consumer protection under the law of negligence
- [ ] Consumer protection under the Consumer Protection Act 1987
- [ ] The rationale for consumer protection under the Consumer Protection Act 1987
- [ ] The limitations on protection given by contract, negligence and the Act

◼ Topic map

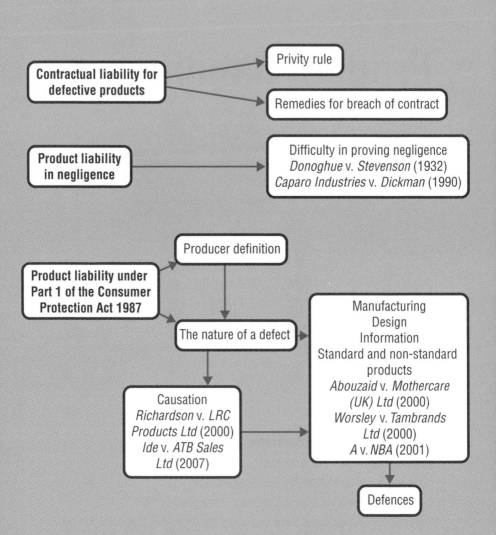

Contractual liability for defective products
- Privity rule
- Remedies for breach of contract

Product liability in negligence
- Difficulty in proving negligence
  Donoghue v. *Stevenson* (1932)
  Caparo Industries v. *Dickman* (1990)

Product liability under Part 1 of the Consumer Protection Act 1987
- Producer definition
- The nature of a defect
  - Causation
    Richardson v. *LRC Products Ltd* (2000)
    Ide v. *ATB Sales Ltd* (2007)
  - Manufacturing
    Design
    Information
    Standard and non-standard products
    Abouzaid v. *Mothercare (UK) Ltd* (2000)
    Worsley v. *Tambrands Ltd* (2000)
    A v. *NBA* (2001)
    - Defences

A printable version of this topic map is available from **www.pearsoned.co.uk/lawexpress**

■ Introduction

The following chapter deals with product liability and its ramifications under the law of contract and negligence, as well as in the Consumer Protection Act 1987.

As a topic in problem questions, assignments and exams, you are expected to demonstrate an awareness and understanding of the different heads of liability and remedies given under each category.

ASSESSMENT ADVICE

Essay questions

Should this topic appear in essay form, you will be expected to compare and contrast the three areas of liability and be able to provide a critical analysis of the advantages and disadvantages of taking actions under each.

Problem questions

A problem question will almost certainly focus on several characters who suffer differing degrees of personal injury and/or property **damage** resulting from a defective product. One will be in a contractual relationship with a retailer who is selling the product on behalf of the producer. The other characters will be victims of 'collateral damage' seemingly caused by the defective product. You will be expected to advise each individual on who is liable for what damage and the nature of the heads of damage that can be claimed.

■ Sample question

Could you answer this question? Below is a typical problem question that could arise on this topic. Guidelines on answering the question are included at the end of this chapter, whilst a sample essay question and guidance on tackling it can be found on the companion website.

PROBLEM QUESTION

Asif is an entrepreneur who owns a large mansion with several acres of land. He often invites his business associates to garden parties. His event organiser, Mona, suggested that he should have a hot air balloon advertising his corporate image at his next party. Asif agreed, so Mona contacted Gas & Air Fun Fair Ltd (GAFF) and asked them to provide a hot air balloon with Asif's logo printed on it.

Asif invited all of his business associates and their families to celebrate 20 years of his company's successful trading. During the party, Ed, an actor, started climbing up the basket's anchor ropes as the balloon ascended. All at once, the valve on the 'burner' jammed and the balloon suddenly plummeted 30 metres or so onto a greenhouse below, damaging several prize orchids, and injuring Babe, a supermodel, who was cut by flying glass.

Both Ed and Babe were taken to hospital. Ed had suffered a broken arm and cannot take up his next film role, while Babe needs plastic surgery to her face that threatens her career as a supermodel.

GAFF refused to accept responsibility. In their view, the hot air balloon had a defect in one of its oxygen canisters, and the injured parties should take up their complaint with the manufacturer, Balloon Air Display Ltd (BAD).

Advise Asif, Ed and Babe as to the suppliers' liability and possible remedies.

Product liability

Consumer protection from defective products is provided under the law of contract, negligence and by the Consumer Protection Act 1987, Part 1.

Contractual protection for consumers

A consumer who suffers loss caused by a defective product can sue for breach of contract terms. Terms can be either expressed (spoken/written) or implied. The most important type of implied terms are those referred to by statute. For instance, the Sale of Goods Act 1979 implies certain key terms into all contracts for sale of goods. These terms (ss. 12–15) cannot be excluded or restricted in any consumer transaction.

✎ EXAM TIP

Read the question carefully. Does it ask for all liability or just liability under the Consumer Protection Act 1987? Where there are several individuals who need to be advised, do not spend too much time on contractual liability at the expense of the other areas of liability.

Similar protection for goods which are transferred as part of a contract of hire or for a service is given to consumers by means of ss. 2–5, Part 1 of the Supply of Goods and Services Act 1982.

📖 REVISION NOTE

The implied terms in contracts for the supply of goods were considered in Chapter 3.

What if a consumer is not a party to a contract?

Consumers who suffer loss caused by someone not in a contractual relationship with them have had to resort to several devices in order to obtain a remedy. This is because the principle of **privity of contract** only allows a person who is party to a contract to enforce rights under that contract. But there are legitimate ways to avoid this principle, such as when one acts as an agent of the buyer, or where the courts construe a collateral agreement.

KEY CASE

Shanklin Pier v. *Detel Products Ltd* **[1951] 2 KB 854**

Concerning: collateral agreements

Facts

The plaintiffs entered into a contract with a contractor to repair their pier and insisted that the defendants' paint be used. The defendants' representative had stated that their paint would last for seven to ten years. But the paint soon deteriorated and the plaintiffs, having to have the pier repainted at extra cost, claimed breach of warranty on the part of the defendants.

Legal principle

There was a collateral contract between the plaintiffs and the defendants because the plaintiffs had shown consideration in stipulating that the defendants' paint had to be used in their joint contract.

> **! Don't be tempted to...**
>
> Don't assume that guarantees override statute. These have been described as worthless. They can be enforced by those who are not party to a contract but may carry terms whereby the consumer has to pay for transporting the goods to the repairer. Be aware of the Sale and Supply of Goods to Consumers Regulations 2002, which state that legal rights are not affected by guarantees and that they must be written in plain, intelligible language.

The Contracts (Rights of Third Parties) Act 1999 has at least gone some way towards alleviating the burden of the privity rule, but in order to enforce such rights, a third party has to be identified or be identifiable as a beneficiary to a contract. Of course, the Act is unlikely to have any impact on consumers.

KEY STATUTE

Contracts (Rights of Third Parties) Act 1999, s. 1

(1) Subject to the provisions of this Act, a person who is not party to a contract (a 'third party') may in his own right enforce a term of the contract if –

    (a) The contract expressly provides that he may, or
    (b) Subject to subsection (2) the term purports to confer a benefit on him.

(2) Subsection (1)(b) does not apply if on proper construction of the contract it appears that the parties did not intend the term to be enforceable by the third party.
(3) The third party must be expressly identified in the contract by name, as a member of a class or as answering a particular description, but need not be in existence when the contract is entered into.

Remedies for breach of contract

Where a contract is breached owing to a defective product, a consumer will want compensation for the loss. The consumer may claim the value of the product and any losses resulting from the breach as long as they are not too remote.

📖 REVISION NOTE

With regard to damages you are advised to refer to the principles of expectation and reliance loss (see Chapter 2) as well as to the rules on remoteness of damage in *Hadley* v. *Baxendale* (see Chapter 5).

The rule of remoteness of damage is crucial to expectation loss and should be highlighted in questions of product liability within a contractual relationship.

Product liability in negligence

Should a consumer suffer loss in a non-contractual relationship, then they could resort to the law of tort by using negligence as a basis for compensation for loss. It should be noted that while obligations in contract are freely undertaken by the parties, obligations in negligence are imposed on the parties by the court. Negligence is based on fault, the principles of which were laid down in *Donoghue* v. *Stevenson* [1932] AC 562.

KEY CASE

Donoghue v. *Stevenson* [1932] AC 562

Concerning: the principles of fault based liability

Facts

Two friends visited a café in Paisley, Scotland, one of whom bought a bottle of ginger beer for her friend, Miss Donoghue. On drinking the beer, Miss D noticed a decomposed snail in the bottle, following which she suffered food poisoning, but was unable to sue the café owner, Mr Minchella, because she had not purchased the product. Instead, she sued the manufacturer, Stevenson, for breaching a duty of care owed to the end user of their product.

Legal principle

Manufacturers owe a duty of care to their customers to ensure that they are not harmed by their product.

The onus of proving fault involves showing: (i) a duty of care owed; (ii) breach of duty; and (iii) foreseeable damage caused; which lies entirely on the claimant and can be difficult to prove. Additionally, there must be no intervening event in the chain of causation. So when liability of manufacturer is an issue, the manufacturer of goods will only be liable when the goods reach the ultimate consumer in the same state as they left the manufacturer.

The difficulty of proving negligence

In establishing negligence the courts will look at the relationship between the parties, the risk involved and public interest factors. There is no simple formula and the law of negligence has developed incrementally to determine the extent of liability.

Caparo Industries v. *Dickman* [1990] 1 All ER 568

Concerning: the extent of a duty of care

Facts

The claimants owned shares in Fidelity. They made a successful takeover of Fidelity based upon the defendant auditor's report. The accounts showed a profit of £1.2m and the claimants alleged they should have shown a loss of £0.4m. The claimants sued the defendants for breach of a duty of care.

Legal principle

There was no duty of care owed to the claimants by the auditors because whether a duty of care is owed depends upon: foreseeability of loss; proximity of relationship; and whether or not it is reasonable to impose such a duty. It was held that not only did the auditors not owe a duty of care to the public, but they did not owe a duty to individual members of the company (relying on a general statement) who wished to buy more shares.

Negligence is difficult to prove because once past the *Caparo* test, the claimant has to show that the duty of care was breached. The final hurdle is presented by a limitation in the damages claimable by virtue of issues such as causation (including multiple causes), remoteness of damage and, finally, by the nature of the damage itself. For instance, claims for economic loss are normally not recoverable unless linked with physical loss or resulting from negligent misstatement.

The need for the Consumer Protection Act 1987, Part I

We have identified the shortcomings of the law of contract and negligence as a way of enforcing consumer rights and seeking a suitable remedy. The Consumer Protection Act 1987 was introduced as a result of the EC Product Liability Directive 85/374/EEC in order to give consumers better protection against damage caused by defective products. Previously, consumers who were non-buyers had to resort to the law of negligence in order to pursue their rights, and buyers who were consumers were often left with no remedy at all should the seller cease trading. The Act allows consumers who suffer loss as a result of a defective product to take action against the producer under what was perceived as a regime of strict liability.

Consumer Protection Act 1987, Part 1, s. 2(1)

… where any damage is caused wholly or partly by a defect in a product, every person to whom subsection (2) … applies shall be liable for the damage.

Producer is defined widely in s. 1(2) of the Act in relation to the product as 'the manufacturer, the abstractor, or processor, who by means of an industrial process changes the essential characteristics of a product'. 'Product' is defined as 'any goods or electricity' including 'a product which is comprised in another product as a component or raw material'. Section 2(2) goes on to extend liability to a range of producers.

Section 2(2) of the Act defines the categories of people who can be held liable under s. 2(1) as:

- A producer of the product.

- An own-brander.

- A business importer of goods from outside the EU.

- Anyone subjecting agricultural produce to an industrial process.

- Anyone extracting raw materials.

It is interesting to note that an industrial process on agricultural produce could include the application of insecticide, fungicide and fertiliser as part of the production process were it to change the 'essential characteristics' of the product.

- Section 2(3) goes on to add that a supplier may find themselves liable if within a reasonable time they do not identify any of the persons listed in s. 2(2) as a source of their product.

✎ EXAM TIP

It is a good idea to show the examiner that you appreciate the rationale behind the Act and the justification for imposing such a high level of liability on the producer.

The nature of product liability

At first hand the liability outlined in s. 2(1) appears to have a simple outcome. It assumes that because liability is strictly interpreted, a producer will be liable for damage caused by defects in their product. However, it is not always easy to prove that there is a defect in a product, and even if there is, that it caused the damage. As a result, Art. 4 of the Product Liability Directive places the burden onto the claimant to prove that a defect caused any resultant damage.

KEY STATUTE

Consumer Protection Act 1987, Part 1, s. 3(1)

... there is a defect in a product ... if the safety of the product is not such as persons generally are entitled to expect.

What are persons 'entitled to expect'? (s. 3(2))

All circumstances should be taken into account including:

- How and why the product was marketed.
- The use of warning marks, instructions about use of the product.
- Reasonable expectations of product use.
- Time of supply by one producer to another.

 Make your answer stand out

It seems that the above definition in s. 3(2) provides the producer with an excuse for what may appear at first hand to be a defective product. Take as an example a beneficial pharmaceutical product with certain damaging side-effects. It could be argued that the safety risks are outweighed by the inherent benefit the product has. In cases like this, the assessment of risk versus benefits involves a 'cost benefit analysis' approach by the courts.

The nature of a defect

The definition given in s. 3 neither outlines a standard model, nor specifies the exact nature of a defect. In fact, subsequent case law has identified various kinds of defect as being the result of manufacturing, design and information failures.

Manufacturing defects

Manufacturing defects will tend to be one-off defects and the result of poor quality control. In such cases, expert evidence becomes a key factor and the judge, who does not have the technical expertise, has to weigh up conflicting evidence and decide which is sound and reliable.

KEY CASE

Richardson v. *LRC Products Ltd* [2000] PIQR 114 (QBD)
Concerning: manufacturing defects

Facts

The claimant became pregnant due to a defective condom. She kept the used condom in a jar in her bathroom cabinet as evidence.

Legal principle

The claimant failed to show that the defect had been caused by the producer. It could have been caused by exposure to ozone after use or during storage.

Design defect

Design defects can have serious implications because they could produce a whole range of defective products.

KEY CASE

Abouzaid v. *Mothercare (UK) Ltd* [2000] EWCA Civ 348
Concerning: design defect

Facts

A 12-year-old claimant was helping his mother attach a sleeping bag to his brother's pushchair when a buckle on one of the elastic straps slipped from his grasp and hit him in the eye, causing him a partially detached retina.

Legal principle

It was proved that due to a design fault the defendants' product had failed to meet the safety standards that the public were entitled to expect.

Information defect

Warnings are necessary when the danger exceeds what the user might reasonably expect. Just as not every aspect of a product may be known, so there is no need to warn the public about every possible danger of a product's use. Only warnings about inherently dangerous products, like that of bleach, need to be given, as well as products that if not used properly might become dangerous.

KEY CASE

Worsley v. *Tambrands Ltd* [2000] PIQR 95 (QBD)

Concerning: information defect

Facts

The claimant suffered toxic shock syndrome which she alleged was caused by a tampon manufactured by the defendant.

Legal principle

Having detailed a warning on a leaflet inside the content's box, it was found that the producer had conveyed all the necessary and relevant information a user needed to know about the product's use.

Standard products and non-standard products

In *A* v. *National Blood Authority* [2001] 3 All ER 298 (see below), Burton J did not favour the traditional categorisation of defects into manufacturing, design and information defects. He preferred to distinguish between *standard and non-standard* products. Burton J suggested that a non-standard product is one which is deficient or inferior in terms of safety from the standard product and it is this deviation from the standard product that has caused the injury. This categorisation goes beyond manufacturing, design or information defects because it covers rogue products which result from the nature of the producer's process. The emphasis on liability also appears to shift from defect to causation.

KEY CASE

A v. *National Blood Authority* [2001] 3 All ER 298

Concerning: standard and non-standard products

Facts

A class action was brought by over 100 claimants who had been infected with hepatitis C after receiving blood transfusions from infected blood products. The National Blood Authority (NBA) claimed they had taken all reasonable precautions in view of the fact that at the time, they did not have the technology to screen blood for the virus.

Legal principle

Finding in favour of the claimants, Burton J held that taking reasonable care was not relevant, as the public were entitled to expect that blood transfusions would be free from infection, even if the risk was unavoidable. The court was concerned with questions of defectiveness, not negligence.

Show how the emergence of a form of strict liability came about in the hepatitis case. The judge did not apply the cost to benefit approach, but assessed the benefits against the risk instead, and in so doing placed the claimants in a win/win position.

Causation

It is clear from s. 2(1) CPA that the consumer must prove on the balance of probabilities that the defect in the product caused the damage.

 Make your answer stand out

It is clear from s. 2(1) of the Act that the consumer must prove on the balance of probabilities that damage was caused by a defect in the product. The case law has shown that this has proved problematic: see *Richardson* v. *LRC Products Ltd* [2000] PIQR 114. Issues of causation are also affected by the defence of contributory negligence, as well as being conditional on a definition of defect from the aspect of 'reasonable expectation entitlement'. Thus, in *Richardson* v. *LRC Products Ltd*, Kennedy J indicated that although a user did not expect a condom to fail, they were not entitled to such an expectation.

Yet a recent decision has indicated that the courts are willing to relieve the consumer to some extent from the burden of proving causation, as the following case illustrates.

KEY CASE

Ide v. *ATB Sales Ltd* [2007] EWHC 1667 (QB)
Concerning: proving the cause of a defect

Facts

The claimant suffered significant brain damage when the handlebar on his mountain bike fractured and injured his head. The defendants argued that the product was not defective, rather the claimant lost control of the bike which resulted in the fracture of the handlebar.

Legal principle

The court held that despite being manufactured to British standards the handlebar was defective within the meaning of s. 3(1). It was not up to the claimant to show *how* the defect had occurred.

KEY DEFINITION: Damage

Damage is defined by s. 5 CPA 1987 as including:

(1) Death or personal injury caused by the defect.
(2) Damage to property (non-business use only) worth more than £275.
(3) Not the damaged product itself.

Defences

The defences are given in s. 4 CPA, the most controversial being the 'development risks defence', because if a product is still on trial and a defect is not discoverable at the time it is put into circulation, then the defendant will not be liable for **damage** caused by its defects. Nevertheless, once a risk becomes known then the defence will not apply, even if the risk is unavoidable. Contributory negligence is provided as a defence according to s. 6(4).

KEY STATUTE

Consumer Protection Act 1987, Part 1, s. 4(1)(a)–(f)

(a) The defect is attributable to compliance with domestic or EC legislation.
(b) The defendant did not supply the product.
(c) The product was not manufactured or supplied in the course of a business.
(d) The defect did not exist at the time the product was put into circulation.
(e) The 'development risks' defence: at the time of manufacture, the state of scientific/ technical knowledge was not such that a producer might be expected to discover the defect.
(f) A supplier of a component will have a defence if the defect was caused by the way it was designed to fit into the manufacturer's product.

Limitation of action

Any action must be brought within three years from the date the damage was caused (or three years from when the damage could reasonably have been discovered), but not more than ten years after the product was brought into circulation.

■Putting it all together

Answer guidelines

See the problem question at the start of the chapter.

Approaching the question

Structure your answer logically, dealing with each party in turn. First, deal with sale of goods liability of GAFF to Asif. Then deal with negligence and product liability to third parties, Ed and Babe, cross-referencing when liability overlaps but applying relevant principles to relevant losses. Don't forget to compare the remedies under each head of liability and reach a balanced, well-argued conclusion.

Important points to include

The following issues are raised:

- Liability of GAFF as supplier under the Sale of Goods Act 1979: breach of implied term of satisfactory quality and remedies/remoteness of damage.

- Liability of GAFF to identifiable third parties.

- Liability of GAFF in negligence.

- Liability of GAFF under relevant sections of the Consumer Protection Act 1987.

- Comparison of measure of damages under each head of liability.

With regard to sale of goods liability to Asif, show that you understand the privity rule by pointing out that only Asif has a claim for faulty goods. Point out that there has been a breach of the implied condition of satisfactory quality under s. 14(2) and fitness for purpose under s. 14(3) SGA 1979. Use relevant authority to support your argument. It is a good idea to deal with remedies for Asif at this point, outlining that he can claim consequential loss subject to the principles of remoteness of damage, viz. the greenhouse and orchids. When considering GAFF's liability to Ed and Babe, mention the privity rule but point out that Ed and Babe may be identifiable third parties under C(RTP)A 1999. Then consider negligence liability before analysing key provisions of CPA 1987, Part I. You will need to identify and explain relevant sections concerning GAFF as producer, defect in the hot air balloon (causal link to damage) and defences for GAFF. Heads of damage for negligence should be distinguished from those awarded under the Consumer Protection Act 1987.

▶

Make your answer stand out

Show your understanding by distinguishing between the heads of liability under contract, negligence and the Consumer Protection Act. Also, by focusing on analysis of defect, you will be able to show your understanding of how problematic and contentious s. 3 CPA 1987 has proved to be in leading cases. Use the case law to identify and explain the difference between design, manufacturing defects and standard and non-standard products. By analysing the requirements for proof of liability under sale of goods, negligence and the Consumer Protection Act 1987 and comparing the different qualification and quantification of damages, you will be in a good position to provide relevant, practical advice as a conclusion.

READ TO IMPRESS

Freeman, R. (2001) Strict Liability Laws – Consumer Protection Act Provisions Fail to Assist Claimants in Three Recent Cases, *Journal of Personal Injury Law* 1.26–36 (Westlaw)

Giliker, P. (2001) Strict Liability Law and the Consumer – A New Era?, *New Law Journal*, 4 May 647–648

Hodges, C. (2001) Product Liability for Old Products, *New Law Journal* 23 March 424–426

Howells, G. and Mildred, M. (2002) Infected Blood: Defect and Discoverability, a First Exposition of the EC Product Liability Directive, 65 *Modern Law Review* 95–106

Mildred, M. (2007) Pitfalls in Product Liability, 2 *Journal of Personal Injury Law* 141–149 (Westlaw)

www.pearsoned.co.uk/lawexpress

 Go online to access more revision support including quizzes to test your knowledge, sample questions with answer guidelines, podcasts you can download, and more!

Product safety

Revision checklist

Essential points you should know:

- [ ] That product safety is covered by criminal liability
- [ ] How the Consumer Protection Act 1987 provides for specific product safety
- [ ] Key provisions under the General Product Safety Regulations 2005
- [ ] Enforcement powers and penalties for both specific and general product safety

Topic map

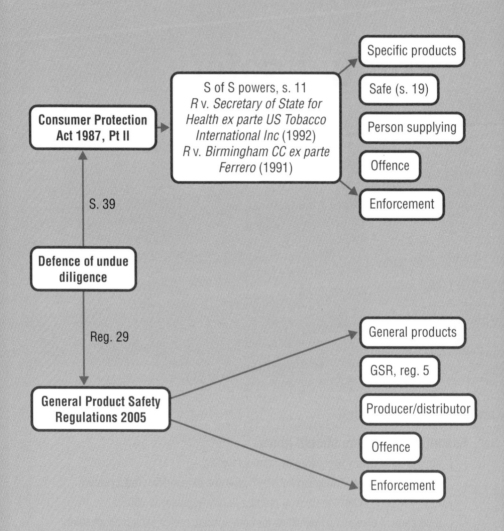

Consumer Protection
Act 1987, Pt II

S of S powers, s. 11
R v. *Secretary of State for
Health ex parte US Tobacco
International Inc* (1992)
R v. *Birmingham CC ex parte
Ferrero* (1991)

Specific products

Safe (s. 19)

Person supplying

Offence

Enforcement

S. 39

Defence of undue
diligence

Reg. 29

General Product Safety
Regulations 2005

General products

GSR, reg. 5

Producer/distributor

Offence

Enforcement

A printable version of this topic map is available from **www.pearsoned.co.uk/lawexpress**

■ Introduction

Products that may have the potential to cause personal injury or death to those who use them are regulated by the Consumer Protection Act 1987, Parts I–V; and the General Product Safety Regulations 2005.

In this chapter, we look at how the law protects users of products by imposing criminal sanctions, not only against producers, but also suppliers of unsafe goods as well.

ASSESSMENT ADVICE

Essay questions

This topic typically lends itself to a comparative analysis of legislation that determines the criminal liability of a producer or supplier. Alternatively, a question may require you to assess the degree of both criminal and civil protection offered to consumers for damage caused by defective products. In which case, you will need knowledge of the topics covered in Chapters 11 and 7 with regard to how relevant provisions of the legislation have been interpreted by the case law – as well as through any current academic argument.

Problem questions

These may take the form of several individual scenarios based on purchasers or users of defective products who suffer injury whilst using them, from which you will be expected to explain and apply salient provisions of legislation and case decisions to the problems presented, and offer further comment if need be.

■ Sample question

Could you answer this question? Below is a typical essay question that could arise on this topic. Guidelines on answering the question are included at the end of this chapter, whilst a sample problem question and guidance on tackling it can be found on the companion website.

ESSAY QUESTION

Critically analyse the different ways in which the criminal law seeks to protect consumers against injury caused by defective products.

Product safety

Prior to the CPA 1987 and the GPS Regulations, consumer safety was governed by the Consumer Safety Act 1978, which was an enabling Act giving the Secretary of State powers to issue regulations to prevent the supply and sale of unsafe goods. This was followed by the Consumer Safety (Amendment) Act 1986, which was intended to prevent unsafe goods – most notably those imported from abroad – from reaching the market by giving customs and trading standards officers powers to detain imported goods, and if necessary, suspend their supply for up to six months, pending an application to the court for forfeiture and destruction.

Consumer Protection Act 1987, Part II

Part II of this Act consolidates the Consumer Safety Act 1978 and the Consumer Safety (Amendment) Act 1986, so as to provide:

- Specific regulations for particular products.
- Various enforcement powers to control trading in unsafe products.
- Civil redress for injured persons on the basis of breach of statutory duty (s. 41(1)).

Specific safety regulations

Section 11 of the Act gives the Secretary of State extensive powers to make regulations concerning specific goods that will effectively:

- Ensure that goods are safe by controlling factors such as their content, design, composition and packaging.
- Restrict their availability for sale.
- Require prescribed information to be supplied with the goods.
- Under s. 11(5), the Secretary of State must consult organisations or persons who are likely to be affected by any proposal he may make.

> **KEY CASE**
>
> *R v. Secretary of State for Health ex parte US Tobacco International Inc* [1992] QB 353
>
> *Concerning: requirement to consult affected parties*
>
> **Facts**
>
> The Secretary of State introduced the Oral Snuff (Safety) Regulations in 1989, without consulting the applicants, who as it happened, were the sole manufacturers and

packagers of snuff in the UK. The Regulations introduced draconian controls on supply and manufacture. Having been encouraged by the inward-investment policy of the government to extend their business into Scotland, the applicants therefore argued that they should have been consulted first.

Legal principle

Given that the company was urged to make a further investment within the UK, they ought to have been given the opportunity to respond to the Secretary of State's proposals. As it stood, the procedure was deemed unfair and so the Regulations were quashed.

Occasionally, there is an urgent need to protect the public and for this reason s. 11(5) allows the Secretary of State to act without consulting any of the affected parties.

KEY CASE

R v. Birmingham CC ex parte Ferrero **[1991] All ER 530**
Concerning: waiver of the requirement to consult affected parties

Facts

Ferrero manufactured chocolate eggs containing small replicas of self-assembly cartoon characters. A child choked to death after swallowing one such component. The council issued a suspension notice stopping the *supply* of eggs for six months. Having tried unsuccessfully to persuade the council to withdraw the notice and accept undertakings not to supply, Ferrero then applied for relief by judicial review. As it was granted, the council appealed on the grounds that they had acted *intra vires* according to s. 11(5).

Legal principle

The appeal was allowed, as a local authority is under no duty to consult a trader either before or after service of a suspension notice.

Note that s. 11(7) excludes drugs and licensed medicinal products which have their own specific legislation.

Items covered by safety regulations

There are a miscellany of products that have been subject to regulation, including children's toys/pushchairs/nightwear/child-proof packaging, as well as such items as car tyres and flammable upholstery.

KEY STATUTE

Consumer Protection Act 1987, Pt II, s. 19

'Safe' is defined in s. 19:

'such that there is no risk or no risk apart from one reduced to a minimum that any of the following will ... cause the death of or any personal injury to any person ...'

Section 19(1)(a)–(e) extends the definition of '**safe**' to include the following list of factors that may cause a product to be deemed unsafe:

- The goods.
- The way they are kept or consumed.
- The way they are assembled – if supplied unassembled.
- Any emissions or leakages from the goods themselves, or as a result of the way they have been kept, used or consumed.
- Reliance on the accuracy of any measurement, calculation or other gauge made by use of the goods.

KEY DEFINITION: Safe

The definition given in s. 19 is concerned only with the dangers posed by goods, and not with their quality. For example, a motor bike might be seen as intrinsically unsafe, but it only becomes unsafe if it has been rendered so by any of the factors mentioned above. Hence the Act seeks to set out minimum, rather than absolute, standards of safety.

The following table gives a practical example of when goods might be considered unsafe under the Act.

Safety factor	Examples of unsafe products
(a) Goods	Faulty bonnet catch on a car
(b) Storage and consumption	Stored safety equipment failing to operate
(c) Assembly	Inadequate instructions or missing items in flat-pack assemblies
(d) Leakages	Emissions from faulty safety caps
(e) Measurements and calculations	Inaccurate gauge settings that might lead to an accident

Breach of safety regulations

Under s. 12 a person commits an offence if he supplies, offers to supply, or agrees to supply, or even just displays for supply; any unsafe goods. Anyone found guilty of breaching these terms can be liable for a fine, or up to six months' imprisonment, or both.

✎ EXAM TIP

Actually, the concept of 'supply' is given wide interpretation by the case law. For instance, in *Drummond-Rees* v. *Dorset CC* (1996) 162 JP 651, the landlord of a holiday home was guilty of *supply*, quite naturally, when he let out his property with unsafe electrical wiring. On the other hand, in *Southwark LBC* v. *Charlesworth* (1983) 147 JP 470, a shoe repairer was found guilty of *supply* when he happened to sell electric fires in the course of his business as a cobbler. It is interesting to note that 'acting in the course of a business' has a less restrictive interpretation in criminal law than that in civil law (see Chapter 1).

Enforcement powers

According to s. 13, the Secretary of State may serve on anyone the following notices:

Notice under section 13	Effect
(1)(a) A prohibition notice	Stops a person from supplying, offering, agreeing to or possessing for supply, any relevant goods deemed by the Secretary of State to be unsafe as described in the notice
(1)(b) A notice to warn	Requires a person at his own expense to publish as specified in the notice, a warning about relevant goods supplied by him which are deemed unsafe by the Secretary of State

Infringement of either of the above notices and the suspension notice described below is an offence which, on summary conviction, carries a penalty of three months' imprisonment, a fine, or both.

Other enforcement agencies include trading standards officers and weights and measures authorities, who are empowered to issue the following notices and orders:

Notice/order	Effect
s. 14: Suspension notice	Prevents disposal of stock for six months on reasonable suspicion that a trader might be supplying goods in breach of a safety regulation. Except, the enforcement authority is liable to compensate the trader should no breach have occurred.
s. 16: Forfeiture order	An application for forfeiture can be made by the enforcement authority to the magistrates' court for unsafe goods to be forfeited. Whereupon they are either destroyed, repaired or salvaged. Trading standards officers can also inspect and seize goods for testing, and examine any associated documents.

▉ General Product Safety Regulations 2005

Prior to these regulations, general product safety was provided by s. 10 CPA 1987 which was replaced by the General Product Safety Regulations 1994. The 2005 Regulations implemented the General Product Safety Directive 95/EC and came into force on 1 October 2005, thereby repealing the General Product Safety Regulations 1994.

> **! Don't be tempted to...**
>
> Don't confuse the GPS Regulations 2005 with the specific product safety regulations provided for by the Consumer Protection Act 1987, Pt II or the General Safety Requirement in the now repealed s. 10.

The General Safety Requirement (reg. 5)

It is an offence for a producer to:

- Place an (unsafe) product on the market.
- Offer or agree to place an (unsafe) product on the market.
- Expose or possess an (unsafe) product for placing on the market.
- Offer or agree to supply an (unsafe) product or expose or possess a product for supply.
- Supply a product that is unsafe.

Producer and distributor (reg. 2)

The Regulations specifically refer to a '**producer**' and a '**distributor**', and as such both terms are given a wide definition.

KEY DEFINITION: Producer and distributor

The definition of a *producer* within reg. 2 bears a marked similarity to that given by the Product Liability Directive, in that it includes a producer as being a manufacturer that can be a re-conditioner, or anyone holding himself out as a manufacturer in the EU. Furthermore, the term 'producer' also includes 'own-branders' and agents as well as importers operating within any EU state. Sometimes a supplier within the distribution chain has an adverse effect on a product's safety, in which case they would be liable as a 'producer' too.

A *distributor* is also a supplier, but can only be made liable if he **knowingly** supplies a product that is patently unsafe.

✎ EXAM TIP

The distinction, then, between 'producer' and 'distributor' relies on the effect of the latter's factoring on the product's safety. A distributor will be termed a 'producer' in circumstances only where he mishandles the safe upkeep of a product he is responsible for distributing.

Duties of a producer (regs. 5 and 7)

Under reg. 5, unsafe products must not be placed on the market by the producer. So far as is practicable, a producer should really give consumers information that will enable them to assess any inherent risks they consider a product may manifest over the course of its normal use; as prescribed by reg. 7.

Duties of a distributor (reg. 8)

Distributors are required to act with due care to make sure that the products they supply are safe. If they are aware or suspect that a product is dangerous, they must not supply it. In any case, the distributor should, within reason, assist in the monitoring of the safety of a product placed on the market.

Product (reg. 2)

Products include second-hand goods, foodstuffs and medicines as well as products supplied for the consumer as part of a service. The Regulation excludes antiques and products that the consumer knows need re-conditioning.

Safe product (reg. 2)

The following definition of safe products is more explicit than that given in CPA 1987, Pt II, as it clarifies the degree of risk that can exist about a product as one which:

- does not present any risk or only minimal risk compatible with its use;
- is acceptable; and
- is consistent with a high standard of health and safety.

Nonetheless, the Regulation does recognise that there is no such thing as an absolutely safe product, but lists the following criteria to determine a product's safety.

Criteria regarding a product's safety

KEY STATUTE

General Product Safety Regulations 2005, reg. 2

'In determining the foregoing the following shall be taken into account in particular –

(a) the characteristics of the product, including composition, packaging, instructions for assembly and ... instructions for installation and maintenance,

(b) the effect of the product on other products, where it is reasonably foreseeable that it will be used with other products,

(c) the presentation ... labelling, warnings, instructions for use and disposal and ... any other information,

(d) the categories of consumer at risk when using the product, in particular children and the elderly.

Application of regulations (reg. 3)

This Regulation states that if a product complies with:

- Specific EU requirements.
- Specific UK law requirements on health and safety.
- A voluntary national standard giving effect to an EU standard.

then the general safety provisions do not apply.

Defences under CPA 1987, Pt II and GPS Regulations 2005

The main defence a trader uses when accused of supplying an unsafe product, is that of due diligence under s. 39 CPA 1987 and reg. 29 GPS Regulations 2005, as outlined opposite.

Often, part of their defence is to blame others in the supply chain for the way they have dealt with the goods.

KEY STATUTE

Consumer Protection Act 1987, Pt II, s. 39 and General Product Safety Regulations 2005, reg. 29

(1) '... It shall be a defence for that person to show that he took all reasonable steps and exercised all due diligence to avoid committing the offence.
(2) Where in any proceedings against any person for such an offence the defence provided ... above involves an allegation that the commission of the offence was due –

   (a) to the act or default of another; or
   (b) to reliance on information given by another ...'

Of course, in order to succeed in the defence a defendant must first identify the other person, and should he base his defence on information provided by another, he must show it was reasonable to rely on it, and that he took reasonable steps to verify its validity. This is stated in CPA 1987, Pt II, s. 39 and GPS Regulations 2005, reg. 29(4)(a), (b).

Penalties

Should an offence be established under regs. 5 or 8(1) of the GPS Regulations, a court can impose one or other of the following penalties:

- A fine not exceeding £20,000.

- Imprisonment for up to 12 months.

Enforcement

Local authority trading standards officers as well as environmental health officers, have powers to monitor and enforce safety standards by issuing the following notices.

Notice	Effect of notice
reg. 11: Suspension notice	Stops a trader from placing a product on the market or supplying it before it is checked
reg. 12: Requirements to mark	Where a product is known to be dangerous, the trader must pay to issue warnings of the risks
reg. 13: Requirements to warn	Should a product pose any kind of category risk, then again, a trader must pay to issue a warning to that effect

▶

Notice	Effect of notice
reg. 14: Withdrawal notice	An enforcement authority can stop a product from being supplied and require the trader to alert consumers of the risk involved
reg. 15: Recall notice	Once a dangerous product is in circulation, an enforcement authority will require a trader to issue a recall notice

As part of their monitoring procedures, enforcement authorities also have powers to make test purchases (reg. 21) and are able to enter and search business premises to inspect any record or product. As a last resort, authorities can also apply to the court for a forfeiture order so that dangerous products can be destroyed (reg. 18).

 Make your answer stand out

When evaluating the extent of protection afforded to consumers by the product safety legislation it would be useful to show that you appreciate that whilst CPA 1987 provides civil redress for breach of statutory duty under s. 41(1), the General Product Safety Regulations provide no such remedy. This is clear by virtue of reg. 42 which clearly states: 'These Regulations shall not be construed as conferring any right of action in civil proceedings in respect of any loss or damage suffered in consequence of a contravention ...' For such infringements, the consumer would have to rely on contractual liability or liability under Part I of the Consumer Protection Act 1987. What is more, there is as yet no equivalent legislation apart from the Supply of Goods and Services Act 1982 and health and safety legislation to ensure safety of services although this is an item for possible reform on the agenda for the European Commission.

■ Putting it all together

Answer guidelines

See the essay question at the start of the chapter

Approaching the question

The question is about protective measures imposed by the criminal Law against injury caused by defective products, so you should focus on the product safety regulations. It might be a good idea to deal with specific product safety regulations provided by Pt II CPA 1987 before tackling the GPS Regulations 2005. Finally, you should undertake a comparative analysis of the degree of protection offered to consumers by each. This should lead you into an effective conclusion which should refer to possible areas for reform.

Important points to include

Start off by defining 'consumer' and stressing the importance of establishing the status of the injured party in terms of ascertaining degree of protection. You should refer to various definitions provided by statutes such as s. 12(1) UCTA 1977 and contrast it with those given in the Unfair Terms in Consumer Contracts Regulations 1999. You should use cases such as *R & B Customs Brokers Co. Ltd* v. *United Dominions Trust* to illustrate how traders have taken advantage of consumer status to gain protection. When dealing with protection under the criminal law, you should give a brief account of the background to the legislation on product safety. You should then focus on s. 11 CPA to define the powers given to the Secretary of State under this enabling Act. Don't forget to use case law such as *R* v. *Secretary of State for Health ex parte Tobacco International Inc.* to illustrate use and abuse of these powers. The definition of 'safe' in s. 19 should be outlined and evaluated using examples. You could leave penalties and enforcement powers until you have dealt with the GPS Regulations. When dealing with the GPS Regulations you need to point out and explain changes such as the division between producer and distributor and the fact that these regulations protect consumers only. Other differences such as the inclusion of second-hand products deserve a mention. When dealing with the definition of 'safe', you should indicate how it differs from that given in CPA 1987. Definitions such as that of 'product' in reg. 2 are worth commenting upon. Turning to penalties, you could point out that penalties are stricter under the GPS Regulations. As regards enforcement, you should describe and explain the different notices/orders and respective enforcement authority and take the opportunity to point out the extra powers of withdrawal and recall given under the GPS Regulations. The defence of due diligence should be referred to before your conclusion, in which you should refer to areas for reform and current programmes of reform.

▶

✓ **Make your answer stand out**

One area that you could elaborate upon is that of the definition of 'product' and the difficulties presented when establishing whether or not a product is 'likely, under reasonably foreseeable conditions, to be used by consumers'. This widens the potential liability of producers in cases where products intended for business use are sold on to consumers. Enforcement also provides an area for contention. It would be useful to refer to journal articles on use of discretion by enforcement authorities in exercise of their powers and why they might be reluctant to use powers such as that of recall.

READ TO IMPRESS

Cartwright, P. (2006) Enforcement, Risk and Discretion: The Case of Dangerous Consumer Products, 264 *Legal Studies* 524–43

Cartwright, P. (2006) Total Recall? The Future of Consumer Product Safety Regulations, *Lloyd's Maritime Commercial Law Quarterly* 390–403

www.pearsoned.co.uk/lawexpress

 Go online to access more revision support including quizzes to test your knowledge, sample questions with answer guidelines, podcasts you can download, and more!

Consumer credit

Revision checklist

Essential points you should know:

- [ ] Methods of providing credit
- [ ] How credit agreements are formed and terminated
- [ ] The licensing arrangements for credit providers
- [ ] How advertising of credit is regulated
- [ ] The principles of enforcement of credit agreements by the creditor

■ Topic map

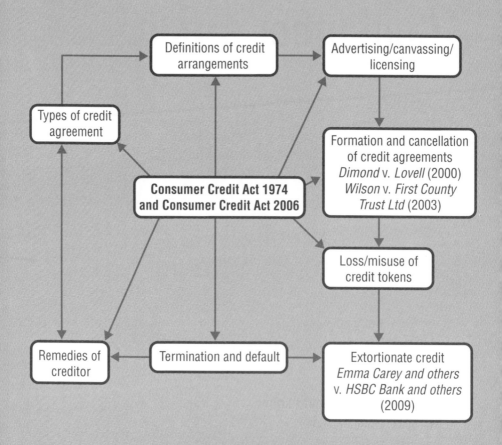

■ Introduction

All businesses and most individuals take out credit in one form or another. Credit is a money-lending service provided by a creditor to a debtor who pays for it in the form of interest.

Because some creditors were inclined to impose severe terms on borrowers, the Consumer Credit Act 1974 was gradually implemented over 11 years to redress inequality of bargaining between consumer debtors and business creditors. It is worth noting that the CCA 1974 is not restricted to protecting consumers, it can protect those who are supplied with credit in the course of a business. Amendments to the CCA 1974 were introduced by the Consumer Credit Act 2006, although some of these reforms have yet to be implemented. In any case, when attempting examination questions, you will be expected to demonstrate knowledge of the nature of these reforms and why they are needed.

ASSESSMENT ADVICE

Questions on credit can take the form of **an essay, a problem, or a series of problem scenarios**. Whilst essays may well focus on evaluation of regulation of consumer credit in general, problems tend to focus on single issues such as formation, termination or remedies for both parties. Whatever form the question takes, you will require detailed knowledge of relevant sections of the current legislation on credit. It is a good idea to make sure you have good knowledge of the reforms effected by the Consumer Credit Act 2006.

■ Sample question

Could you answer this question? Below is a typical problem question that could arise on this topic. Guidelines on answering the question are included at the end of this chapter, whilst a sample essay question and guidance on tackling it can be found on the companion website.

PROBLEM QUESTION

Nick, a double glazing representative for Fullglaze Ltd, called on Faith at her house and persuaded her to enter into a credit sale agreement to finance replacement windows and doors in her home. The total price was £7,200, payable in 48 monthly instalments ▶

of £150. In his eagerness to keep an appointment with another potential customer, Nick entered an incorrect figure on the agreement for the cost of credit. Faith and Nick signed both copies and he gave her a copy together with notice of her cancellation rights. Four days later, on Friday, Faith changed her mind and wished to cancel the agreement. She phoned up Fullglaze Ltd to inform them of her change of mind and was told to send a letter of cancellation to Head Office immediately. Faith sent an email instead but it was not accessed until the following Tuesday.

Fullglaze are insisting that Faith is bound by the agreement and are threatening to take legal action against her.

Advise Faith.

Types of credit transactions

It is useful to look at the main forms of credit provision before examining the protective measures given by the Consumer Credit Act 1974.

Hire purchase

Under a hire purchase agreement a debtor hires goods for a fixed time period by regular payment instalments and then is given the option to buy them, for a token sum of money, at the time of the last instalment. Hire purchase is popular with creditors as they can recover goods easily when the hirer fails to pay, because ownership of the goods does not pass until the option to purchase has been exercised. The owner of the goods tends to be a specialist finance company which buys them from the supplier to hire to the debtor.

Conditional sale

As with hire purchase, ownership of property does not pass until all payment instalments have been made. However, in conditional sales, the debtor must buy the goods at the end of the term: they are not given the option. Conditional sales tend to be confined to the purchase of industrial plant and equipment.

Credit sale

Ownership of goods passes to the buyer (debtor) immediately, at the time of the contract or delivery, so that the buyer is provided with credit to allow time to pay. The buyer, as owner, can sell the goods or dispose of them before the end of the repayment agreement, as long as all outstanding amounts of credit are paid off.

Loans

A creditor lends money to a debtor so that the debtor can buy goods or services and the debtor repays the loan with interest over a period of time. Loans can be offered with or without security and secured loans may take the form of a registered charge over assets, or a third party guarantee. An unsecured loan can be made in the form of an overdraft facility provided by a bank or a personal loan, but interest on an overdraft facility is usually higher than that on a loan.

Credit cards

The holder of a credit card is given a credit limit and can use the card to buy goods, services, or cash advances. When a debtor pays a supplier by credit card, the supplier forwards details of the purchase to a credit card company which pays the supplier after deduction of a charge between 1% and 4%. The debtor receives a monthly account of spending with a request for a minimum amount that must be paid. If the debtor pays the amount in full, there is no interest charge, although any cash advance given is always subject to interest charges.

Trade credit

It is customary for traders to defer payment for goods or services and this type of credit is not subject to the protection offered by the Consumer Credit Act 1974. Small businesses, however, can gain some protection from the Late Payment of Commercial Debts (Interest) Act 1998 (see Chapter 5).

■ Consumer Credit Acts 1974 and 2006

The Consumer Credit Act 1974 is the main statute governing credit and provides for both civil and criminal liability. Before addressing the provisions of the Act, it is essential that the following definitions of credit arrangements are understood.

Regulated agreement

A definition of a **regulated agreement** is given in the Consumer Credit Act 1974.

KEY STATUTE

Consumer Credit Act 1974, s. 189(1)

'regulated agreement' means a consumer credit agreement, or consumer hire agreement, other than an exempt agreement ...

As the section refers to **consumer credit agreement**, consumer hire agreement and exempt agreement, these terms need to be explained.

Credit agreement

> **KEY DEFINITION: Consumer credit agreement**
>
> Section 8(1) states: 'a consumer credit agreement is an agreement between an individual (the debtor) and any other person (the creditor) by which the creditor provides the debtor with credit of any amount.'

An individual can be a person, a small partnership (two or three people) or an unincorporated association. For agreements created before 6 April 2008, a consumer credit agreement was limited to £25,000, excluding charges such as interest. Since 6 April 2008, this financial restriction has been removed by the Consumer Credit Act 2006. The following case shows the difference between a consumer credit agreement and a consumer hire agreement.

> **KEY CASE**
>
> ***Dimond* v. *Lovell* [2000] 2 All ER 897**
>
> *Concerning: the difference between a consumer credit agreement and consumer hire agreement*
>
> **Facts**
>
> L drove into the back of D's car and D hired a replacement car from 1st Automotive Ltd who specialised in hiring cars out in accidents without requesting payment until claims were settled. L's insurer – Cooperative Insurance Society (CIS) – refused to pay the hire charge of £364.63 because they claimed that the contract between D and 1st Automotive was an unenforceable consumer credit agreement and in any case, D had not mitigated her loss.
>
> **Legal principle**
>
> The House of Lords found that the agreement between D and 1st Automotive was a regulated consumer credit agreement and unenforceable because it infringed the CCA 1974. It was not a regulated consumer hire agreement because it was not capable of lasting more than three months. As the contract was illegal, neither Mrs D nor L's insurer had to pay for the hire car.

Consumer hire agreement

Section 15 of the CCA 1974 gives a definition of a consumer hire agreement.

KEY STATUTE

Consumer Credit Act 1974, s. 15

(1) A consumer hire agreement is an agreement made by a person with an individual (the 'hirer') for the bailment of goods to the hirer, being an agreement which –

(a)   is not a hire-purchase agreement, and
(b)   is capable of subsisting for more than three months, and
(c)   does not require the hirer to make payments exceeding [£25,000].

EXAM TIP

It may be a good idea to let the examiner know that you are aware that the £25,000 financial limit does not apply to agreements made on or after 6 April 2008.

The agreement must be *capable* of running for more than three months, so it can still be a consumer hire agreement if it actually runs for less than three months. Likewise, as long as the hirer is not required to pay more than £25,000, it can still be a consumer hire agreement if actual payment exceeds £25,000. Remember, the £25,000 limit only applies to contracts made before 6 April 2008.

Exempt agreement

Exempt agreements are not regulated agreements and are listed as follows:

■ Mortgage loans provided by building societies, local authorities and other non-profit making organisations to develop land.

■ Low cost credit in debtor-creditor agreements offered to a limited class of individuals where the interest rate does not exceed the bank's rate +1% or 13%, whichever is the higher.

■ Fixed sum debtor-creditor-supplier agreements (not conditional sale or hire purchase) where the maximum number of payments is four within 12 months.

■ Credit card purchases where the account must be settled in full with one payment within a certain time.

EXAM TIP

It is worth pointing out that, since 6 April 2008, high-net-worth debtors and agreements relating to businesses can be exempted from most of the CCA 1974. The debtor or hirer has to be a natural person (not a partnership) of high-net-worth and must make a declaration agreeing to forgo the protection of the CCA 1974 (see s.16A). Likewise, ▶

a debtor or hirer who makes agreements mainly for their business, trade or profession, may find that their agreement is exempt (see s. 16B). The effect of these provisions is to remove credit protection for rich individuals and those who borrow for business purposes. However, a small degree of protection is offered by way of the unfair credit relationship provisions with regard to extortionate credit.

More definitions

Sections 10 and 11 of the amended CCA 1974 give further definitions of credit transactions which are summarised in the table below.

Consumer Credit Act 1974 (amended) section number	Credit transaction
Section 10: **Running-account credit** and fixed-sum credit	Running-account credit agreements allow for separate contracts and can run indefinitely, as long as the debtor makes regular monthly repayments and does not exceed a credit limit, for example, a Visa credit card
	Fixed credit agreements have their credit set at a fixed sum and it will be discharged once this sum has been paid off, for example, a bank loan
Section 11: **Restricted-use credit** and **unrestricted-use credit**	Restricted-use credit is transferred from the creditor to the supplier of the debtor's goods and services, for example, hire purchase and conditional sale agreements as well as credit card transactions
	With unrestricted-use credit, the money is given to the debtor personally, even if granted for a specific purpose

Debtor-creditor-supplier agreements

A debtor-creditor-supplier or DCS agreement is one in which the creditor is the supplier of goods or services, or where the creditor has or intends to have a business connection with such a supplier. Section 12 of the amended 1974 Act defines three types of DCS agreement, as follows:

■ Restricted-use credit where the creditor is the supplier, e.g. credit sales.

- Restricted-use credit where the creditor has an existing or proposed future arrangement with a supplier, e.g. payment by credit card.

- Unrestricted-use credit where the creditor has a pre-existing arrangement with a supplier, and knows that the loan is to finance a transaction between debtor and supplier. This is rare, because a creditor would be more likely to transfer the money directly to the supplier making it a restricted use arrangement, as described in the point above.

Debtor-creditor agreements

Here there is no connection between the creditor and supplier of goods and services and CCA 1974 does not apply to the agreement between the supplier and debtor.

✎ EXAM TIP

It is essential that you understand the difference between DCS and DC credit agreements, because where there is a business connection between a creditor and supplier, both supplier and creditor will be liable to the customer for potential misrepresentations and breaches of contract by the supplier.

❗ Don't be tempted to...

Don't forget, a credit agreement can be a multiple agreement. Usually, restricted-use credit transactions will be DCS agreements and unrestricted-use transactions will be DC agreements. So, credit sales and hire-purchase will be restricted-use DCS agreements. Credit cards are combination agreements because if they are used to obtain a cash loan, they are unrestricted-use credit under a DC agreement. However, should the credit card be used to pay for goods and services, they transform into restricted-use DCS agreements under s. 12(b) CCA 1974.

Non-commercial agreements

CCA 1974 does not extend to **non-commercial agreements**, such as those between family members.

KEY DEFINITION: Non-commercial agreement

A consumer credit or hire agreement not made by a creditor or owner in the course of a business carried out by him.

The following case clarified the meaning of 'in the course of a business'.

KEY CASE

Hare v. *Schurek* **[1993] CCLR 47**

Concerning: the meaning of 'business' in the definition of non-commercial agreements

Facts

The claimant was a car dealer who did not normally provide credit to his buyers but on one occasion he decided to supply a car to a friend on hire purchase terms. The question arose as to whether or not he needed a licence under the Consumer Credit Act 1974.

Legal principle

The Court of Appeal decided that as the claimant did not operate a consumer credit or hire business, the agreement was not made in the course of a business and being non-commercial according to the CCA 1974, no credit licence was required.

Advertising, canvassing and licensing of credit

The aim of the controls on advertising and canvassing is to promote truth in lending and to encourage customers to 'shop around' for credit.

Advertising

Advertising of credit is controlled by the Consumer Credit (Advertisements) Regulations 2004 which aim to ensure that consumers are supplied with enough information to enable them to make an informed choice. All advertisements should therefore use plain and intelligible language, be legible or audible and state the name of the advertiser. Also, if the consumer's house is required for security, a specifically worded warning should be printed in the advertisement.

Canvassing (s. 48 CCA 1974)

Canvassing involves making unsolicited oral representations off trade premises to try to persuade a consumer to enter into a regulated agreement. So, if a credit provider visits a customer at any trade premises or responds to a home visit request from a customer, they are not canvassing for credit. The table opposite outlines the controls on canvassing.

Total prohibition on canvassing off trade premises	No total prohibition on canvassing off trade premises
Debtor-creditor agreements (cash loans)	Other credit agreements
Criminal Offence under s. 49 even if solicited, unless signed request in writing from customer	Doorstep promotion of credit for goods and services with specific canvassing licence
	Bank employees can canvass for overdraft facilities in customer's home

Licensing

There are several categories of business activity which need a credit licence, including consumer credit and hire businesses, credit brokerage, debt adjusters and counsellors, debt collectors and credit reference agencies. The Office of Fair Trading regulates the conduct of those who are licensed to provide credit and anyone in default can be subject to a civil fine of £50,000. Offering credit without a required licence is a criminal offence and agreements made by an unlicensed trader are generally unenforceable against a debtor.

Criminal offences

The following offences are provided by CCA 1974, ss. 45–51:

- Advertising restricted-use credit for goods and services without offering them for cash.

- False or misleading advertisements for credit.

- Canvassing of DC agreements off trade premises.

- Soliciting a DC agreement off trade premises in response to a request that is not in writing or signed.

- Sending circulars to minors to invite them to borrow money, obtain goods or services on credit or hire, or apply for information or advice on borrowing, credit or hire.

- Giving a person an unsolicited credit token.

Formation of a consumer credit agreement

Before entering into a consumer credit agreement, a customer must be given pre-contract information in a separate document, otherwise the agreement will be unenforceable without a court order. Regarding antecedent negotiations, CCA 1974 recognises that these may involve several parties and makes provision for this in s. 56. Section 56 defines antecedent negotiations as:

- Creditor negotiating with debtor.

- Credit-broker negotiating with debtor regarding goods sold or to be sold to the creditor with a view to a DCS agreement.

- Supplier negotiating with debtor or hirer regarding a DCS agreement.

Antecedent negotiations are deemed to start when the negotiator and the debtor or hirer first enter into communication.

Withdrawal from prospective agreements

Section 57 allows a person to withdraw from a prospective regulated agreement and any linked transactions such as insurance, or installation or servicing of goods, by giving oral or written notice to anyone acting as a negotiator.

Making the agreement

An agreement must contain 'key financial information', 'other financial information' and 'key information' as stipulated by the Consumer Credit (Agreements) (Amendment) Regulations 2004. Furthermore, s. 60 CCA 1974 lists the required form and content of agreements which, if not adhered to, will result in the agreement being seen as improperly executed (s. 61). Until an agreement is signed by both parties, it is unexecuted. Sections 62 and 63 describe the duty to supply copies of unexecuted and executed agreements respectively and to let the debtor know of any rights to revoke and cancel the agreement. The duty to supply copies of agreements with notice of cancellation rights does not apply to non-commercial agreements, overdrafts on current accounts, or small DCS agreements for restricted-use credit (up to £50).

Improper execution of the agreement

Prior to CCA 2006, some improperly executed agreements could not be enforced.

KEY CASE

Wilson v. *First County Trust Ltd* [2003] UKHL 40

Concerning: unenforceable credit agreement owing to improper execution

Facts

A debtor took out a loan using her car as security. However, there was a mistake in the agreement about the amount of credit.

Legal principle

The agreement was unenforceable under s. 127(3)–(5) CCA 1974 because it had been improperly executed.

Because of litigants like Mrs Wilson, who enriched themselves by means of debt avoidance on technical grounds, s. 127 was amended by the CCA 2006, so that a court now has discretion to decide whether or not to grant an enforcement order in such cases.

KEY STATUTE

Consumer Credit Act 1974, s. 127

(1) In the case of an application for an enforcement order under –

(a)   Section 65(1) (improperly executed agreements) . . .

The court shall dismiss the application if, but only if, it considers it just to do so having regard to –

(i) prejudice caused to any person by the contravention in question, and the degree of culpability for it . . .

✎ EXAM TIP

When examining the rules for formation of credit agreements it is useful to point out that the amendments introduced by the 2006 Act mean that a court now always has the power to enforce an agreement under s. 127(1) and (2). Thus, cases like *Wilson* v. *First County Trust* and *Dimond* v. *Lovell* would be decided differently now, so that litigants can no longer be unjustly enriched because of minor technical infringements of the rules.

Cancelling a regulated agreement

A regulated agreement may be a **cancellable agreement** if it is cancellable according to s. 67 CCA 1974.

KEY DEFINITION: Cancellable agreement

This is an agreement signed by a debtor away from the trade premises of the creditor or supplier which may be cancelled as long as it was not secured on land.

The policy behind cancellable regulated agreements is to discourage high-pressure doorstep selling. Section 68 of the 1974 Act provides a cooling-off period of five clear days (14 in some circumstances) from receipt of the copy of a signed cancellable agreement. This means that the debtor can cancel the agreement as long as it is in writing and the cancellation is effective as soon as posted.

Liability of the supplier and creditor

The creditor will be liable for any misrepresentations or breaches of contract made by the supplier by virtue of ss. 56 and 75 of the 1974 Act.

CCA 1974 section no.	Provision of section
Section 56: Antecedent negotiations	Any credit broker or supplier who negotiates with a debtor will be seen to be acting as the agent of a creditor
Section 75: Liability of creditor for breaches by supplier	The creditor is jointly liable with the supplier for any misrepresentation or breach of contract as long as the agreement is: – A regulated credit agreement – Relates to an item of cash price £100–£30,000 – The credit is provided under an agreement between creditor and supplier

Important points about s. 75

- The creditor and supplier must be different persons.

- Any exclusions of liability for breach and misrepresentation that apply to the supplier, apply to the creditor too.

- As the creditor and supplier *are jointly and severally liable*, either or both can be sued.

- Does not apply to non-commercial agreements.

- Only applies to purchases bought with credit card, rather than debit or cheque guarantee card.

- Applies even where debtor exceeds credit limit.

- Applies to goods supplied using part credit and part cash. The creditor is liable to refund the whole amount (credit and cash).

- It is not possible to contract out of s. 75.

It was argued that equal liability did not apply to overseas transactions made by UK card holders, however in *OFT* v. *Lloyds TSB Bank plc* [2006] 2 All ER 821 the Court of Appeal held that s. 75 does apply to transactions made abroad using UK-issued credit cards.

Loss or misuse of credit tokens

A definition of credit tokens is given by s. 14(1).

KEY STATUTE

Consumer Credit Act 1974, s. 14(1)

A credit token is a card, cheque, voucher, coupon, stamp, form, booklet or other document or thing given to an individual by a person carrying on a consumer credit business, who undertakes –

(a) that on the production of it ... he will supply cash, goods and services ... on credit, or

(b) that where, on the production of it to a third party ... the third party supplies cash, goods and services ... he will pay the third party for them ... in return for payment to him by the individual.

A debtor is not liable for a credit token until it has been accepted either by signing it, signing a receipt for it, activating it, or using it. Once a credit token has been accepted, then the debtor must give notice to the issuer when the card has been lost, stolen or misused. Until notice is given, the debtor remains liable for any loss arising. Although notice can be given orally, the credit agreement may stipulate that written notice must be given within seven days of verbal notification.

Extent of debtor's liability for lost, stolen or misused credit tokens before notice given

Circumstances of loss	Debtor's liability
Card given to misuser with debtor's consent	Debtor has unlimited liability
Card obtained by misuser without owner's consent	Debtor liable for £50 only or the credit limit – whichever is the lower
Card used fraudulently in distance selling transaction	Debtor not liable for loss and is entitled to cancel the payment or a re-credit if payment has been made (Consumer Protection (Distance Selling) Regulations 2000)

Extortionate credit terms

CCA 2006 repealed the extortionate credit provisions in ss. 137–140 CCA 1974 and replaced them with new unfair relationship provisions in ss. 140A–140C. Sections 140A and 140B apply to unregulated as well as regulated agreements. When determining whether or not a debtor/creditor relationship is unfair, under s. 140A, a court will consider:

- the nature of the terms;

- the manner in which the creditor has exercised his rights; or

- any other thing done by or on behalf of the creditor, before or after the agreement.

KEY CASE

Emma Carey and others v. *HSBC Bank and others* **[2009] EWHC 3417 QB**

Concerning: temporarily unenforceable agreement not rendering a relationship unfair

Facts

A bank failed to supply a debtor with the required copy of a loan agreement within a stipulated time period of 12 days. The debtor claimed that the relationship was unfair because of this omission on the part of the bank.

Legal principle

Although the bank's failure to execute the agreement properly made the agreement temporarily unenforceable, it did not render the relationship unfair.

! Don't be tempted to...

Don't suppose that a court will readily assume an unfair relationship under s 140A. Each case is decided on its own facts but it is apparent that there has to be some evidence of bad faith, such as failing to state who has been paid commission or misleading borrowers into paying personal protection insurance as a mandatory condition for taking out a loan.

On finding that an unfair relationship exists, a court may, on application by the debtor, issue an order under s. 140B, which empowers it to:

- Order repayment of any sum paid by a debtor or surety.

- Order a creditor to do or refrain from doing anything specified in the order.

- Reduce or discharge any sum payable by the debtor or surety under the agreement.

- Direct the return of property taken as security under the agreement to a surety.

- Set aside, partly or wholly, any duty imposed on the debtor or surety under the agreement.

- Alter the terms of the agreement or any related agreement.

- Direct accounts to be taken between any persons (the court is allowed to ask for accounts to be kept of any credit payments made by the debtor to the creditor or anyone authorised by the creditor to collect payment).

Termination and default

A debtor may wish to terminate an agreement by paying the debt off early, or may default owing to change in financial circumstances, in which case the creditor may wish to terminate the agreement.

Early settlement by the debtor

Regulated consumer credit agreement	Hire purchase and conditional sale
CCA 1974, s. 94(1): Debtor can settle the debt at any time by giving written notice to the creditor	CCA 1974, s. 99(1): Debtor can terminate the agreement by giving written notice to creditor
CCA 1974, s. 95: Debtor will be entitled to a rebate on interest	CCA 1974, s. 99(2): Debtor must pay arrears and unless a lower termination price or no price is stipulated in the agreement, will have to bring payments up to half the total price (s. 100(1))
	CCA 1974, s. 100(4): Debtor must compensate creditor for loss caused to the goods

Termination by the creditor

Although some agreements allow a creditor to terminate an agreement at will when the debtor becomes unemployed or is convicted of dishonesty, in most cases a creditor terminates an agreement owing to the debtor's default.

Default

A default notice must be served on the debtor if the creditor wishes to end the agreement, recover possession of goods or land, or enforce any security (s. 87). The default notice has to explain the breach, and what is required to put it right. If the breach cannot be rectified, the creditor should state how much compensation is required and by what date, as well as the consequences of non-compliance. The debtor should be given seven days in order to comply with the default notice.

Where the debtor remedies the breach, it is treated as not having occurred, but if the debtor ignores the notice, the creditor can terminate the agreement.

Repossession of goods under hire purchase and conditional sale

Although the property in the goods remains with the seller under hire purchase and conditional sale agreements, s. 90 provides that a creditor must obtain a court order to enter premises to repossess goods from a debtor who has paid one third of the total price by the time of the breach.

KEY STATUTE

Consumer Credit Act 1974, s. 90(1)

At any time when –

(a) the debtor is in breach of a regulated hire-purchase or a regulated conditional sale agreement ... and

(b) the debtor has paid to the creditor one-third or more of the total price of the goods and

(c) the property in the goods remains in the creditor,

the creditor is not entitled to recover possession of the goods ... except on an order of the court.

EXAM TIP

Section 90 stopped the practice of 'snatch back' by creditors who, formerly, would repossess goods from defaulting debtors at any stage of the agreement. Now, any creditor who breaches s. 90 faces severe penalties in that the agreement will be terminated, and the debtor will be freed from all liability and will be able to recover from the creditor all sums paid under the agreement (s. 91).

! Don't be tempted to...

Don't mix up early settlement with repossession. Be careful not to make the mistake of thinking that s. 90 applies where a debtor has exercised a right of termination of a hire purchase or conditional sale agreement. In such cases, as outlined above, ss. 99–100 apply to cover the obligations of the debtor.

Remedies of the creditor

Apart from exercising rights to terminate a credit agreement or repossess goods under a hire purchase or conditional sale agreement, a creditor can also take an action for arrears (an agreed sum) or damages against a debtor who breaches an agreement.

Action for arrears

Although a creditor has the right to sue a debtor for arrears, CCA 1974 safeguards the consumer's interests as follows:

■ The rate of interest payable on arrears should be no more than the rate for the total charge for credit (s. 93).

■ The court may make a time order under s. 129.

■ The creditor must give the debtor notice before demanding early payment of any sum under s. 87 (see above).

■ The court may re-open an extortionate credit bargain under s. 140B (see above).

Time orders

A time order can be granted where a creditor brings an action to enforce a regulated agreement, to repossess goods or land, or take any security. Upon receiving a default notice, a debtor or hirer may apply for a time order as long as 14 days' notice of the application is given to the creditor. A time order usually applies to sums owed, but with hire purchase and conditional sales it can apply to sums payable under the agreement.

Damages

The measure of damages in the case of early termination of a hire purchase or conditional sale agreement differs according to who terminated the agreement.

Termination of hire purchase/ conditional sale agreement by *debtor*	Termination of hire purchase/ conditional sale agreement by *creditor*
Creditor can sue for damages: Measure of damages is calculated according to s. 100(1) so that the debtor has to pay a sum to make up 50% of the total cost of the goods + any installation costs in full, unless the court is satisfied that the creditor's loss is less than this sum (s. 100(3))	Where the creditor terminates owing to debtor's breach (but not repudiation): Creditor can claim for arrears + interest + any amount needed to compensate for damage to the goods Cannot normally claim for loss of a bargain, unless the creditor makes the ▶

Termination of hire purchase/ conditional sale agreement by *debtor*	Termination of hire purchase/ conditional sale agreement by *creditor*
Goods must be returned to the creditor	broken term an essential term of the contract – in which case the contract will be deemed to be repudiated by the debtor and the creditor may be allowed to claim for loss of bargain
	Goods can be repossessed by creditor

□ REVISION NOTE

Using the common law, a creditor can always make it an essential term of the agreement that the debtor pays instalments on time and, if not, treat the contract as repudiated by the debtor. If the agreement is repudiated by the debtor's breach, then it is the debtor who is terminating the agreement by breaching an essential term, thus entitling the creditor to claim damages for loss of a bargain. You may wish to refer to Chapter 2 for the common law rules on classification of terms and measurement of loss.

KEY CASE

Lombard North Central v. *Butterworth* [1987] 1 All ER 267

Concerning: repudiation by the debtor by breach of an essential term

Facts

A term in a contract for the hire of computers stated that prompt payment of all instalments was essential. The defendant breached this term by making several late payments and the creditor terminated the agreement and claimed damages for loss of the whole contract (loss of bargain).

Legal principle

Because the term was described as an essential term, its breach amounted to repudiation by the defendant and so the creditor had the right to terminate the agreement and claim damages for loss of a bargain.

! Don't be tempted to...

It is easy to mistake an action for an agreed sum for an action for damages. They are different. In an action for an agreed sum a person will sue for an amount agreed in the contract, such as the price. In a credit sale, an agreed sum would be the credit provided plus interest, which may involve claiming for arrears. Actions for damages, on the other hand, are subject to the common law contractual rules on remoteness of damage, measure of loss and mitigation.

■ Putting it all together

Answer guidelines

See the problem question at the start of the chapter.

Approaching the question

The question concerns an improperly executed credit agreement made off trade premises and related rights of cancellation. You may also mention that it is possible that Nick is canvassing for credit. As well as explaining the implications of improperly executed agreements and the right to cancel, you also need to advise Faith on the basis that she may be bound by the agreement, in which case you will need to explain remedies available to Fullglaze.

Important points to include

- Identify the agreement as a debtor-creditor-supplier restricted-use credit agreement and explain what this means.
- Deal with the canvassing issue and apply and explain the provisions in s. 48 CCA 1974.
- Improper execution: explain the provisions in CCA 1974 on formation of credit agreements: ss. 60, 61, 62 and 63. Then explain how s. 127 CCA 2006 has reformed the requirements for properly executed agreements by giving judges the discretion to uphold improperly executed agreements.
- Rights of cancellation: identify the agreement as an off trade premises agreement and explain the cancellation rights under s. 67 CCA 1974. Apply the cooling-off ▶

period (described in s. 68) to the scenario and address the issue of an emailed cancellation notice to decide whether or not Faith has cancelled the agreement.

■ In the event of Faith being bound by the agreement, explain the remedies available to Fullglaze: action for arrears (s. 86).

 Make your answer stand out

With regard to improper execution of agreements, explain that the amendments regarding execution of agreements aim to deter persistent litigants, like Mrs Wilson, from profiting from minor technical infringements in the execution of credit agreements thereby enriching themselves by means of debt avoidance on technical grounds. Summarise the judgments in cases like *Dimond* v. *Lovell* and *Wilson* v. *First County Trust*. Then explain how s. 127 was amended to give judges the discretion to uphold improperly executed agreements. Point out that the amended s. 127 is wide enough to empower a court to ignore technical infringements made by mistake, but enforce an agreement where technical infringements have been deliberate. With regard to the cooling-off period, it is questionable whether five clear days after receipt of the agreement or notice of statutory cancellation rights is long enough and perhaps it should be extended.

READ TO IMPRESS

Dobson, P. (2006) Consumer Credit Act 2006, *Student Law Review* 49 Autumn

www.pearsoned.co.uk/lawexpress

 Go online to access more revision support including quizzes to test your knowledge, sample questions with answer guidelines, podcasts you can download, and more!

Agency law

■ Topic map

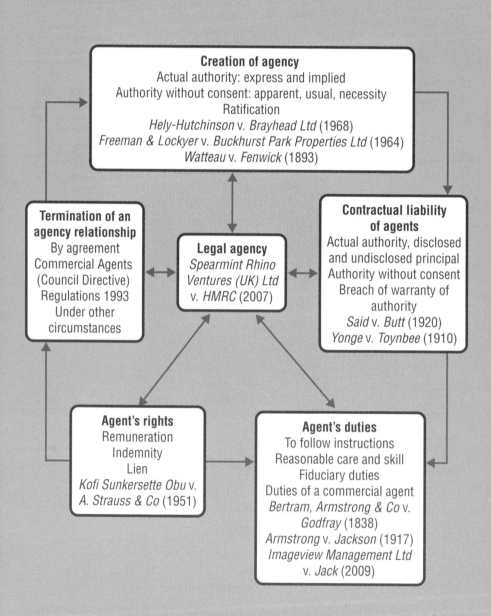

Creation of agency
Actual authority: express and implied
Authority without consent: apparent, usual, necessity
Ratification
Hely-Hutchinson v. *Brayhead Ltd* (1968)
Freeman & Lockyer v. *Buckhurst Park Properties Ltd* (1964)
Watteau v. *Fenwick* (1893)

Termination of an agency relationship
By agreement
Commercial Agents (Council Directive) Regulations 1993
Under other circumstances

Legal agency
Spearmint Rhino Ventures (UK) Ltd v. *HMRC* (2007)

Contractual liability of agents
Actual authority, disclosed and undisclosed principal
Authority without consent
Breach of warranty of authority
Said v. *Butt* (1920)
Yonge v. *Toynbee* (1910)

Agent's rights
Remuneration
Indemnity
Lien
Kofi Sunkersette Obu v. *A. Strauss & Co* (1951)

Agent's duties
To follow instructions
Reasonable care and skill
Fiduciary duties
Duties of a commercial agent
Bertram, Armstrong & Co v. *Godfray* (1838)
Armstrong v. *Jackson* (1917)
Imageview Management Ltd v. *Jack* (2009)

A printable version of this topic map is available from **www.pearsoned.co.uk/lawexpress**

◼ Introduction

Businesses often use an intermediary to carry out commercial activities on their behalf. Such intermediaries act as agents for a business by marketing products or negotiating contracts for sale or purchase.

However, care should be taken when using the term 'agent' because the law attaches special significance to the relationship of agency. In respect of this relationship, the *principal* has responsibility over the actions of the *agent*, and so anything undertaken by the *agent* will bind the *principal* to compliance with the outcome of any dealings with a *third party*.

ASSESSMENT ADVICE

The most likely question on the conceptual analysis of agency is upon the extent of an agent's authority and the effects of any contractual transaction undertaken by an agent whilst exercising that authority. These notions of agency can be quite complex and call for clear analysis of the various permutations of authority. Plan your answer by first drawing a chart to illustrate the alternating engagement of authority before starting to write, so as to disentangle the relationship between the parties involved.

◼ Sample question

Could you answer this question? Below is a typical problem question that could arise on this topic. Guidelines on answering the question are included at the end of this chapter, whilst a sample essay question and guidance on tackling it can be found on the companion website.

PROBLEM QUESTION

Pat owns a health club and employs Al as her general manager. Al's duties include ordering supplies for the club including food and drink for the bar. She also allows several fitness instructors to use her facilities to run classes. All of the instructors use the equipment provided by the club, although they are not required to wear the club uniform. Pat pays the instructors according to the number of weekly classes they hold. ▶

Advise Pat as to her liability for payment in the following situations:

(a) She has received a demand from Her Majesty's Revenue and Customs for payment of VAT for services provided by her fitness instructors.

(b) TP Supplies Ltd has sent Pat an invoice for payment of £500 for the supply of nuts and crisps for the bar. On enquiring who had ordered these supplies, Pat discovered that it was Al, despite being given strict instructions only to buy fresh fruit and healthy food for the bar. Al was also instructed not to buy nuts in view of possible allergies on the part of customers.

Legal agency

An agent acts as an appointee of a principal mostly to negotiate contractual relations between the principal and a third party. Recognised agency relationships may include those between directors and their company, or partners and their fellow partners. Quite often people call themselves agents because they sell a certain brand of product which they have purchased from the producer of the brand. This does not constitute a relationship of legal agency, since the product has been bought and sold on by the purchaser – who has acted on his own behalf and not that of the branded producer.

KEY DEFINITION: An agent

He who acts through another, acts for himself – *qui facit per alium, facit per se.*

KEY CASE

Spearmint Rhino Ventures (UK) Ltd v. *HMRC* **[2007] EWHC 613 (Ch)**

Concerning: when an agent is really a principal

Facts

The defendant (Spearmint Rhino Ventures (UK) Ltd) contested a tribunal decision for the claimant (HMRC) that they had directly supplied the services of lap-dancers as agents. HMRC held that, by exercising control over service fees that the dancers received from customers – for dances and 'sit-downs' – Spearmint Rhino was liable for consideration of VAT.

Legal principle

Although the dancers paid a trade commission to Spearmint Rhino, they were acting as *principals* in their own right by separately negotiating whatever fee their services to customers might render. So, the dancers were not engaged as Spearmint Rhino's agents, since they entertained the customer on their own behalf, and were themselves liable to account for VAT for services they performed.

Make your answer stand out

What is made clear by recent case law (see *Kieran Mullen Ltd* v. *CEC* [2003] STC 274 and, more pertinently, *Portman Escort Agency* v. *Customs & Excise* [2006] UKVAT (Excise) is that the degree of control over services to the customer does not have to be a crucial factor in determining whether agency actually exists at all. It now seems that greater emphasis is placed upon the financial accountability of whoever performs the service.

Creation of agency

An agent can only act on behalf of a principal if he has the authority in law to do so. How that authority is acquired will determine the extent to which an agent's acts will bind a principal. Authority may be granted with or without the consent of a principal.

Authority with consent

Authority given with consent is often referred to as 'actual authority' and may be express or implied.

Express actual authority

Written or verbal agreements between an agent and a principal denote express, actual authority and the agreement is usually contractual, but need not be so. For instance, an agent who agrees to act for no fee provides a gratuitous, rather than contractual, service.

Implied actual authority

Implied actual authority arises out of the relationship between an agent and a principal, or as a result of each other's conduct.

KEY CASE

Hely-Hutchinson v. *Brayhead Ltd* [1968] 1 QB 549

Concerning: implied actual authority by conduct

Facts

Mr Richards was the chairman of a company whose directors allowed him to act as if he was the managing director as well. Without any stated authority, he entered into a contract on behalf of the company to act as a guarantor for a third party's debts. Understandably, the company wanted to avoid the contract of guarantee that Mr Richards had made on its behalf. ▶

Legal principle

The company was bound by the contract, as it had by conduct granted Mr Richards the implied authority of a managing director.

✎ EXAM TIP

A quote from the case may prove useful in demonstrating your understanding of the concept of implied actual authority. A good example from the *Hely-Hutchinson* case would be that given by Lord Denning: 'It is implied when it is inferred from the conduct of the parties and the circumstances of the case ...' In the *Hely* case, Lord Denning stated that Mr Richards was authorised 'to do all such things as fall within the usual scope of that office'.

It follows from Lord Denning's comments that an agent has the implied authority to do everything necessary to follow the principal's instructions unless, of course, such acts are expressly forbidden to those who are granted actual authority in the first place.

KEY CASE

Waugh v. *H. B. Clifford and Sons Ltd* [1982] 2 WLR 679

Concerning: use of implied authority by an agent to ignore the principal's express instructions

Facts

A firm of builders who were being sued in negligence employed solicitors to defend their case. When the solicitors reached a compromise settlement, the builders instructed the solicitors not to compromise 'at any cost'. These instructions were ignored by the solicitors, who nevertheless entered into a compromise agreement.

Legal principle

Although solicitors, as agents, have implied actual authority to enter into compromise agreements, this does not of course apply when they have been expressly instructed otherwise by their clients.

Authority without consent

Authority without consent is also referred to as apparent or ostensible authority.

Apparent authority

Apparent or ostensible authority is not the result of an agreement between an agent and principal, but emerges when a principal indicates to a third party by statement or implication that an agent has the authority to act on behalf of the principal. When a third party gains such an impression from the principal and acts in reliance on that impression, then the principal may be prevented *(estopped)* from denying that the agent has *his* apparent authority.

KEY CASE

Freeman & Lockyer v. *Buckhurst Park Properties Ltd* **[1964] 2 QB 480**

Concerning: estoppel

Facts

The directors of a company allowed K to act as if he was the managing director. He then engaged a firm of architects on behalf of the company, whom the company refused to pay.

Legal principle

The company was liable because the directors had given the impression that K was empowered to make contracts on the company's behalf: 'The representation which creates apparent authority may take a variety of forms … the commonest is by conduct' (per Lord Diplock).

For apparent authority to operate, three criteria must be satisfied:

- Representation by the principal.
- Reliance on the part of the third party.
- Unawareness on the part of the third party.

✎ EXAM TIP

Expand your explanation of Lord Diplock's statement on 'representation' in *Freeman & Lockyer* by pointing out that by allowing a person to carry out the executive actions of an agent vicariously, the principal is allowing the third party to assume that the person has 'actual' authority.

! Don't be tempted to…

Do not assume that the third party has to be disadvantaged by some kind of loss when he acts in reliance on the principal's representation that the agent has actual authority. Actually, the only disadvantage a third party can suffer is by entering a contract as a result of a false impression given by a principal.

Sometimes the court expects a third party to be alerted to an agent's possible lack of authority.

 Make your answer stand out

Ascertaining the third party's awareness about the limits of an agent's authority can be problematic, because the court sometimes assumes that a third party should, in fact, be alert under certain circumstances to an agent's lack of authority. You need to explain to the examiner that a court will take into account any behavioural facts as witnessed from a third party's point of view. As it stands, case law cannot predict a third party's awareness about an agent's lack of authority, as is indicated by the two cases outlined below.

It is interesting to compare and contrast the decisions in the following cases.

KEY CASE

Lloyds Bank Ltd v. *The Chartered Bank of India, Australia and China* [1929] 1 KB 40
Concerning: the third party's awareness of agent's lack of authority

Facts

A bank's employee paid cheques, obtained fraudulently from his employer, into the defendant bank under his own name. The defendant bank claimed they were not liable to reimburse the principal bank for the cheques.

Legal principle

The defendant bank were liable because they should have been 'put on notice' as to the number of fraudulent cheques that happened to be signed by the same employee of the principal bank.

KEY CASE

First Energy (UK) Ltd v. *Hungarian International Bank Ltd* [1993] 2 Lloyd's Rep 194
Concerning: where a third party should be alert to lack of authority of an agent

Facts

A senior manager, J, at a bank told the claimants that he did not have authority to grant them credit. Thereafter, he falsely told the claimants that Head Office had given their approval for them to be given credit. The bank claimed that they were not bound by the contract made by J because the third party was aware of J's lack of authority.

Legal principle

The bank was bound by the contract made by J. Although the claimants knew that J lacked authority to allow credit, the bank had implied that J did have authority for communicating the bank's decisions to all third parties.

Usual authority

There is another kind of *authority* which is an extension of *implied and apparent* authority that does suggest a category of authority in its own right as it is linked to a trade practice as a recognised course of dealing. The following cases provide examples of *usual authority*.

KEY CASE

Panorama Development (Guildford) Ltd v. Fidelis Furnishing Fashions Ltd [1971] 2 QB 711

Concerning: usual authority arising out of apparent authority

Facts

A company secretary hired cars for his own use in the defendant's name. Having not been paid, the car hire company (third party) sued the defendant company for payment as they had denied all liability.

Legal principle

The company secretary had *apparent authority* to carry out administrative tasks from which *usual authority* was granted to him for hiring cars as part of his job. Consequently, the company was bound by contracts entered into by the company secretary in pursuance of his recognised role.

The following case provides an example of usual authority as a category of authority in its own right.

KEY CASE

Watteau v. Fenwick [1893] 1 QB 346

Concerning: usual authority as an independent category of authority

Facts

The owner of a public house sold it to brewers who then retained the former owner as the manager. The manager kept his name as licensee and agreed with the brewers to buy only bottled beer and mineral water. Although this agreement also prohibited the purchase of tobacco products, the manager ordered cigars from a supplier (third party), who then had to pursue the brewers for non-payment.

Legal principle

The brewers were liable as a principal even though they expressly forbade the purchase of tobacco products in the agreement they had with the manager, who himself had no apparent authority (as an agent) since he had not disclosed that he was acting for a principal.

Make your answer stand out

In *Watteau* v. *Fenwick*, the manager had neither actual express nor implied authority to buy cigars. In fact, he was expressly forbidden to buy tobacco products. What is more, the manager could not claim apparent authority, because the principal – being undisclosed – had never held out that the manager was his agent for this contract. Despite not realising that the manager was an agent, the third party was, however, entitled to assume that the manager had the authority to enter into contracts usual for a person in his position.

! Don't be tempted to…

Don't assume that the *Watteau* case will always be exercised, since the circumstances in which *Watteau* will apply are restricted to the following criteria:

1. the agent has no actual authority because he has been forbidden to carry out an act by the principal;
2. the third party must be unaware of the existence of a principal and think that the agent is acting on his own behalf; and
3. the agent must make a contract which is usual for an agent in his position.

Agency by necessity

In extreme circumstances the law will either impose an agency relationship upon parties or extend an existing relationship to include the following mutually inclusive conditions:

- The agent must be in control of the principal's property.
- Obtaining the principal's instructions would be impossible.
- A real emergency exists.
- The agent must act in good faith.

KEY CASE

Springer v. *Great Western Railway Co* [1921] 1 KB 287

Concerning: agency of necessity

Facts

A strike at a dockyard delayed the delivery of a consignment of tomatoes. As they had started to perish, the agent felt he had to sell them.

> **Legal principle**
> Because the agent could have contacted the principal for instructions, this was not seen as an agency of necessity.

✎ EXAM TIP

It may be useful to point out that an agency of necessity is less likely to arise these days owing to advanced means of communication that offer agents and principals no excuse for being uninformed about one another's likely reasons for action.

Agency by ratification

Usually, an agent receives the authority to act as an agent of the principal before he so acts. Conversely, the principal's ratification creates a principle of volition subsequent to the agent's action. Moreover, when a principal ratifies an agent's act, the ratification is effective from the date of the agent's act rather than from the date of the ratification. Even so, five conditions need to be satisfied in order for ratification by the principal to be effective:

- The agent must claim to be acting for the principal so the principal must be named or be able to be identified, as an **undisclosed principal** cannot ratify an agent's actions.

- The principal must have had full capacity to make the contract at the time of the agent's act. In the landmark case of *Boston Deep Sea Fishing and Ice Co Ltd* v. *Farnham* [1957] 1 WLR 1051 the court held that ratification of an agent's action by the principal was not possible, because at the time of the agent's action the principal was an enemy alien and therefore lacked the capacity to enter into such a contract.

- At the time of ratification, the principal must either have known all of the material facts or have had every intention to ratify the action, irrespective of what the facts were.

- A void contract cannot be ratified.

- Ratification must also take place within a reasonable time of the agent's agreement with the third party.

■ Liability for contracts made by an agent

Actual authority

Where an agent acting on actual authority makes a contract on behalf of a **disclosed principal**, then usually the principal rather than the agent is bound.

KEY DEFINITION: Disclosed and undisclosed principal

A principal is *disclosed* when he is named or when the agent indicates that he is acting on behalf of a principal, whereas a principal is *undisclosed* when the agent does not reveal that he is acting on behalf of a principal.

If an agent does not disclose that he is acting on behalf of a principal when entering into a contract then the contract will be struck between the agent and the third party, so that each incurs liability towards the other. Once the principal is subsequently disclosed, the third party will incur liability to the principal, and should the agent have actual authority, both agent (A) and principal (P) will be jointly liable to the third party (TP). This can be represented schematically as follows.

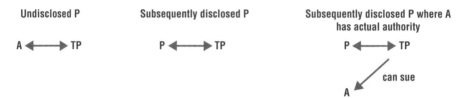

Cases where a subsequently disclosed principal cannot sue on a contract

The principal, once disclosed, cannot sue the third party in the following situations:

- Where a relationship of agency is excluded by a contract term.
- Where the third party would not have contracted with the undisclosed principal.
- Where the third party intended to contract with the agent personally.

KEY CASE

Said v. *Butt* [1920] 3 KB 497

Concerning: loss of a principal's right to sue a third party

Facts

Said, a theatre critic, wanted to attend the first night of a play. Knowing that the theatre owners would not sell him a ticket, he asked a friend to buy him one. On trying to attend the opening night, Said was refused entry, which left him with no alternative but to sue the theatre owner.

Legal principle

The theatre owner was not liable as a third party to Said because had he known that the ticket was to be given to Said, he would not have sold it to Said's friend – who acted as agent. Therefore, he was within his rights to refuse Said entry.

In the absence of actual authority

Were an agent to act without actual authority on behalf of an undisclosed principal, no liability will attach to the principal unless the rule of usual authority, as outlined in *Watteau* v. *Fenwick*, applies. Of course, ratification does not apply when the principal is undisclosed because the agent does not act as an agent, but acts on his own behalf instead.

Breach of warranty of authority

When an agent falsely informs a third party that he has authority to act for a principal, he may cause the third party to act to his own detriment; in which case, the agent will be liable for breach of warranty of authority. Furthermore, an agent can also be liable for breach of warranty even if he exceeds his authority innocently.

KEY CASE

Yonge v. *Toynbee* **[1910] 1 KB 215**

Concerning: breach of warranty of authority

Facts

The principal (Yonge) instructed his solicitor (Toynbee) to defend a case, yet unbeknown to the solicitor, Yonge had become insane.

Legal principle

As soon as the principal was certified as insane, the solicitor had no authority to act for him and so became liable from the time of the principal's insanity for the claimant's costs (third party).

Exceptions to agent's liability for breach of warranty of authority

There are three circumstances in which an agent will not be liable for breach of warranty of authority.

- Where the principal ratifies the agent's acts.
- If the third party knew or ought to have known of the agent's lack of authority.
- Where the agent denies having authority or if the third party did not rely on the agent having authority.

Summary of liability on contracts made by agents

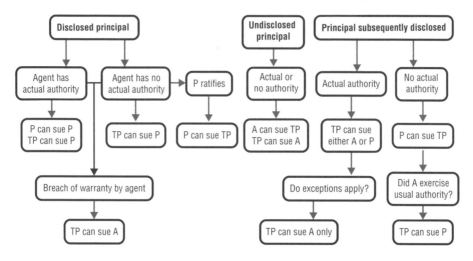

■ The duties of an agent

As the relationship between a principal and agent is based on trust and confidence it is by nature **fiduciary**. There are several duties owed by an agent to a principal that can arise either out of the fiduciary relationship or the agency agreement itself.

The duty to follow instructions

As long as the principal's instructions are clear the agent has to follow them precisely.

KEY CASE

Bertram, Armstrong & Co v. *Godfray* [1838] 1 Knapp 381

Concerning: duty to follow the principal's instructions

Facts

An agent failed to follow his principal's instructions to sell shares at a certain price because he thought the price would increase. Unfortunately, the share price fell.

Legal principle

The agent was liable and had to pay the principal damages for failing to follow his instructions.

The duty to use reasonable care and skill

An agent must use reasonable care and skill in carrying out his duties. This is supported by the following implied statutory term.

Supply of Goods and Services Act 1982, s. 13

In a contract for the supply of a service where the supplier is acting within the course of a business, there is an implied term that the supplier will carry out the service with reasonable care and skill.

The degree of care and skill required depends upon the expertise an agent claims to possess. For instance, a solicitor acting as an agent will be expected to demonstrate the standard of care and skill reasonably expected of a solicitor.

Fiduciary duties

An agent has three important fiduciary duties:

- To avoid conflicts of interest.
- Not to make secret profits or take bribes.
- To be able to account for any payments received.

Conflicts of interest

An agent should not put himself in a position in which his interest conflicts with his duty. There must be no conflicts between his interests and those of the principal.

Armstrong v. *Jackson* [1917] 2 KB 822

Concerning: conflict of interest

Facts

A stockbroker acting on the instructions of his principal bought 600 shares in a company. As it was, the stockbroker (agent) already owned the 600 shares and merely transferred them to his principal.

Legal principle

Here the stockbroker had placed himself in a position where his duty conflicted with his own interest.

An agent can avoid a conflict of interest by disclosing the conflict to the principal, thereby giving the principal the opportunity either to appoint another agent, or consent to the agent acting on his own behalf as well as for himself, as in the case of a solicitor who is able to act for both parties in a transaction.

KEY CASE

Clark Boyce v. *Mouat* [1994] 1 AC 428

Concerning: consent to conflict of interest

Facts

A solicitor acted for both a mother and son in a mortgage transaction. Actually, the mother had wished to secure a mortgage on her house in order to give her son a loan.

Legal principle

This arrangement was lawful because a solicitor may act for both parties in a transaction even if the interests of the parties conflict, provided that he gains the informed consent of both parties.

Secret profits

A secret profit arises when an agent receives profit over and above that agreed with the principal, whilst acting for the principal. There are two surreptitious ways in which a secret profit can arise:

- By means of an agent's act alone.
- With the help of a third party in the form of a bribe.

KEY CASE

Imageview Management Ltd v. *Jack* [2009] EWCA Civ 63

Concerning: secret profit made by an agent

Facts

An agent negotiated the transfer of a goalkeeper, Kevin Jack, to Dundee United for 10% of the player's salary, while at the same time agreeing a separate, undeclared deal with the club for arranging a work permit for the player. Realising that his agent had made a secret profit, the player stopped paying his agent 10% of his salary, and sued him for non-disclosure.

Legal principle

The footballer's agent was not entitled to a fee for obtaining a work permit as well as his 10% remuneration, since he had breached his fiduciary duty by making a secret arrangement with the club.

If an agent takes a bribe from a third party, the principal may countenance certain options. In dismissing the agent, he can recover any commission already paid to the agent. He is also entitled to recover the bribe from the agent or third party and hold it on trust for himself. In addition, instead of recovering the bribe he can sue the agent or third party to remedy his losses and have the contract made with the third party rescinded.

Duty to account

The property of the agent must be kept separate from that of the principal unless the agreement says that both may be mixed. Once more, accurate accounts of any transactions between the parties must be kept by the agent and be available for inspection by the principal.

Duties of a commercial agent

A commercial agent is one who negotiates the sale or purchase of goods for a principal or who acts on the principal's behalf to conclude a contract for sale or purchase of goods. A statutory definition is given below.

KEY STATUTE

Commercial Agents (Council Directive) Regulations 1993, reg. 2(1)

'commercial agent' means a self-employed intermediary who has continuing authority to negotiate the sale or purchase of goods on behalf of another person (the 'principal'), or to negotiate and conclude the sale or purchase of goods on behalf of and in the name of that principal …

In acting on behalf of a principal, the commercial agent must act dutifully and in good faith. In carrying out such duties, the agent must make every effort to negotiate and if necessary conclude transactions as reasonably instructed by the principal, as well as communicate to the principal all necessary information.

■ Rights of an agent against a principal

Apart from having obligations towards a principal, an agent is entitled to demand the right to remuneration, or to be **indemnified**, and hold the right to impose a lien on the principal's property.

Remuneration

The right to receive remuneration arises only if there is an express or implied term in the agent's contract. Such a term is implied by statute.

Supply of Goods and Services Act 1982, s. 15

(1) Where under a contract for the supply of a service, the consideration for the service is not determined by contract, left to be determined in a manner agreed by the contract or determined by the course of dealing between the parties, there is an implied term that the party contracting with the supplier will pay a reasonable charge.

(2) What is a reasonable charge is a question of fact.

✎ EXAM TIP

Take the opportunity to explain and comment upon this section by stating that it operates where a contract is silent about payment or method of payment for a service, leaving it to be determined by course of dealing or trade practice. You may wish to observe that the use of the word 'reasonable' in sub-section (1) will be linked to parties' expectations in light of the transaction in question. Also, sub-section (2) is less than helpful in that it adds an element of unpredictability to assessing a suitable remuneration by always making it case-specific.

Any express term about the amount of remuneration contained within an agency contract will, of course, supersede an implied term, even that of s. 15.

KEY CASE

Kofi Sunkersette Obu Appellant v. *A. Strauss & Co* [1951] AC 243

Concerning: express term on remuneration overrides implied term

Facts

An agency contract contained an express term outlining the level of remuneration to the agent as well as a term saying that extra remuneration was payable as commission *at the principal's discretion*. In the event, the principal refused to pay the agent commission.

Legal principle

The agent was not entitled to receive commission because the contract contained an express term stating that it was payable at the principal's discretion.

! Don't be tempted to...

Don't assume that although an express term may specify an amount of remuneration, a term can be implied into a contract to ensure fulfilment of a transaction in order that an agent receives due payment. The following case refused to imply such a term into an agency agreement.

KEY CASE

Luxor (Eastbourne) Ltd v. *Cooper* [1941] AC 108

Concerning: refusal to imply a term into a contract to fulfil an express term

Facts

An estate agent was promised by the vendor (principal) of two cinemas a £10,000 commission on completion of sale so long as they found suitable buyers. The agent duly found two suitable buyers, but the vendor changed his mind and refused to complete. The agent sued the vendor (principal) for breach of an implied term that stipulated that he would allow the sale to be completed.

Legal principle

The term could not be implied as the inflated commission was payable on completion of the sale rather than on the introduction of prospective buyers. Anyway, part of an estate agent's trade practice is to accept the risk of losing a sale before completion.

 ## Make your answer stand out

Perhaps the above decision would have been different if the express term had stated that £10,000 would have been payable on finding a prospective purchaser willing to complete the sale. See *Dashwood (formerly Kaye)* v. *Fleurets Ltd* [2007] EWHC 1610 QB.

Indemnity

In the absence of an alternative agreement an agent is entitled to be indemnified for liability of his agency business. This right is lost should he exceed his duty or act negligently.

Lien

In the event of a breach of the agency contract by the principal, the agent can hold onto but not sell or dispose of any of the principal's goods that are in his possession. It is worth noting that a lien cannot be exercised by the agent if it is forbidden by the agency contract.

■ Termination of an agency agreement

When a principal ends the agreement between himself and his agent, it will inevitably have an effect upon third parties who deal with the agent. Although a principal can withdraw authority from the agent at any time, if he does so, he must inform the third party as well, to avoid giving the impression that the agent has apparent authority to act on his behalf. There are various ways in which an agency agreement can be ended.

Termination by agreement

Non-contractual agency agreements can be terminated at any time. However, the termination of a contractual agreement will depend upon whether or not the agreement is for a fixed term. Fixed term agreements will automatically expire once the fixed term for their duration has lapsed. Nevertheless, it is often the case that agency agreements do not stipulate a time period, in which situation there are two possible methods of termination:

■ Implication of automatic termination by reference to trade custom.

■ Termination by reasonable notice.

 Make your answer stand out

Point out that although the term 'reasonable notice' is case-specific, the Commercial Agents (Council Directive) Regulations 1993 do stipulate minimum requirements for reasonable notice (see below).

Termination under the Commercial Agents (Council Directive) Regulations 1993

According to reg. 15, minimum notice periods apply to agencies of indefinite duration as follows:

Length of agency	Minimum notice period
Up to one year	One month
Up to two years	Two months
After two years	Three months

Note: These notice periods do not apply when the contract is terminated on account of either party's breach or in exceptional circumstances.

Obviously, the principal and agent can agree to longer periods of notice if needs must. It is interesting to note that the above minimum periods of notice will also apply where an agency agreement has continued even after expiry of a fixed term.

Compensation and indemnity under the Regulations (reg. 17)

Either compensation or indemnity is payable to a commercial agent on termination of the agreement, but unless the agent chooses indemnity, compensation will be awarded as a matter of course.

Compensation

Regulation 17(6) states that compensation is available for damage suffered as a result of termination of the agreement. This could include damage due to loss of commission expected from performance of the contract.

Indemnity

Indemnity is based on the benefits given by the agent to the principal as explained in reg. 17(3).

KEY STATUTE

Commercial Agents (Council Directive) Regulations 1993, reg. 17(3)

… the commercial agent shall be entitled to an indemnity if and to the extent that –

(a) he has brought the principal new customers or has significantly increased the volume of business with existing customers and the principal continues to derive substantial benefits from the business with such customers; and

(b) the payment of this indemnity is equitable having regard to all the circumstances and, in particular, the commission lost by the commercial agent on the business transacted with such customers.

The amount of indemnity can not exceed the agent's average annual commission paid over the previous five years (reg. 17(4)).

Loss of the right to compensation and indemnity (reg. 18)

The right to compensation and indemnity is lost in the following situations:

- On justifiable termination of the contract by the principal for breach by the agent.
- Where the agent, having full mental and physical capacity, terminates the contract in the absence of breach by the principal.
- Where the agent, with consent of the principal, assigns his duties to another agent.

Termination in other circumstances

Automatic termination of the agency contract will take effect in the following cases:

- Frustration of contract.
- Death of either party.
- Insanity of either party.
- Bankruptcy of the principal.
- Bankruptcy of the agent – where it interferes with his ability to act for the principal.

■ Putting it all together

Answer guidelines

See the problem question at the start of the chapter.

Approaching the question

This question assesses your knowledge and understanding of two areas of agency: (a) the legal existence of an agency relationship; and (b) the nature of authority granted to an agent by the principal.

Important points to include

In part (a) you should highlight the difficulty in establishing whether or not an agency relationship exists. VAT cases such as *Kieran Mullen* v. *CEC* (2003) and *Spearmint Rhino Ventures (UK) Ltd* v. *HMRC* provide ample material for your analysis.

In part (b) you need to explain the principle of actual authority, implied actual authority and usual authority arising out of apparent authority (*Panorama Development (Guildford) Ltd* v. *Fidelis Furnishing Fashions Ltd* (1971)).

You should also address the effects of the contract in view of the fact that the principal in this case is unlikely to ratify the agreement.

 Make your answer stand out

For part (a), point out that recent case law makes it very clear that the fact that a principal exercises a high degree of control over the purported agent does not necessarily indicate a relationship of agency. You could also suggest that in the scenario, if the fitness instructors negotiate their own fees with Pat, then they could be seen as acting on their own behalf. You may well wish to question the policy behind decisions such as those given in *Kieran Mullen* and *Spearmint Rhino*. As regards part (b), when discussing apparent authority, you should analyse cases like *Lloyds Bank Ltd* v. *The Chartered Bank of India, Australia and China* (1929) to ascertain whether or not TP Supplies Ltd should have been alert as to Al's lack of authority to buy unhealthy or allergy inducing snacks for a health club.

READ TO IMPRESS

Brown, I. (1995) The Agent's Apparent Authority: Paradigm or Paradox, *Journal of Business Law* 360

Dowrick, F. E. (1954) The Relationship of Principal and Agent, 17 *Modern Law Review* 24

Flannigan, R. (2008) The (Fiduciary) Duty of Fidelity, 124 *Law Quarterly Review* 274

Reynolds, F. M. B. (1969) Personal Liability of an Agent, 85 *Law Quarterly Review* 92

www.pearsoned.co.uk/lawexpress

 Go online to access more revision support including quizzes to test your knowledge, sample questions with answer guidelines, podcasts you can download, and more!

Liability for unfair trading practices

Revision checklist

Essential points you should know:

- [ ] The aims of the Unfair Commercial Practices Directive 2005/29/EC
- [ ] What constitutes an unfair commercial practice under the Consumer Protection from Unfair Trading Regulations 2008
- [ ] The range of defences offered to a trader under CPUTR 2008
- [ ] The degree of protection offered to businesses from unfair trading practices

■ Topic map

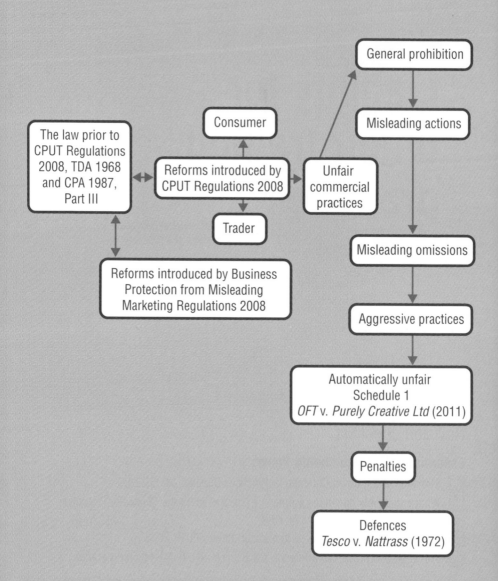

◼ Introduction

The law of unfair trading is concerned with protecting the interests of honest customers and traders, by imposing criminal sanctions, enforceable by public authorities, on traders who offer a sub-standard service.

Needed reform has bolstered criminal liability for unfair trading practices by introducing new offences under the Consumer Protection from Unfair Trading Regulations 2008. The Regulations also enable enforcement authorities to obtain enforcement orders, thereby avoiding the requirement for a prosecution.

ASSESSMENT ADVICE

Essay questions

For this type of question, endeavour to explain and comment on any of the main concepts introduced by the Consumer Protection from Unfair Trading Regulations. For more in-depth analysis, distinguish between key provisions of the Trade Descriptions Act 1968 and the Consumer Protection from Unfair Trading Regulations.

Problem questions

A problem question is likely to expect you to apply the provisions of the Consumer Protection from Unfair Trading Regulations to a case scenario. As yet, there is no case law emanating from the new Regulations, so you will need to show detailed knowledge of these provisions and their possible implications for future cases.

◼ Sample question

Could you answer this question? Below is a typical problem question that could arise on this topic. Guidelines on answering the question are included at the end of this chapter, whilst a sample essay question and guidance on tackling it can be found on the companion website.

PROBLEM QUESTION

Miss Fit owns a hotel which offers 'Tone-up Weekend Breaks' for clients who wish to improve their health and fitness. The hotel brochure lists a swimming pool, sauna, steam room and a hot tub amongst their amenities. Worryingly, she received a letter of complaint from Max Moan, who claimed that he was unable to use some of these facilities over the weekend of his stay. Certainly the hot tub had been closed for cleaning, and worse still, the pool was out of use due to its closure by Environmental Health. Consequently, Mr Moan is threatening to report the hotel to the OFT.

What advice would you give to Miss Fit regarding:

(a) Criminal liability for unfair trading practices.
(b) Any possible defences available to her.
(c) Powers of enforcement available to public authorities such as the OFT.

■ The law before the Consumer Protection from Unfair Trading Regulations 2008

Before the introduction of the 2008 Regulations it was recognised that many customers were reluctant to enforce their civil rights against traders who made false or misleading descriptions of goods or services. Consumers and even businesses often lacked the sheer tenacity to pursue a civil remedy because of the cost, delay and complexity of dispute procedures. This allowed unscrupulous traders to get away with low standards of service. The Trade Descriptions Act 1968 protected both consumers and businesses from false and misleading descriptions by imposing *criminal* sanctions on 'rogue traders'. Misleading pricing was provided for under Part III of the Consumer Protection Act 1987. Both of these Acts have now been abrogated by the Consumer Protection from Unfair Trading Regulations 2008, which introduced consumer protection measures against a wider range of unfair trading practices.

Offences under the Trade Descriptions Act 1968

The Act created two strict liability offences under s. 1 that applied to traders making false or misleading descriptions about products. Services were covered by s. 14 which unlike s. 1 required a degree of *mens rea* in the form of knowledge or recklessness.

False statements about goods	False statements about services
Section 1(1): Any person who in the course of any trade or business – (a) applies a false trade description to any goods; or (b) supplies or offers to supply any goods to which a false trade description is applied: shall … be guilty of an offence.	Section 14(1): It shall be an offence for any person in the course of any trade or business – (a) to make a statement which he knows to be false; or (b) recklessly make a statement which is false; as to … (i) The provision in the course of any trade or business, of any services.

The intention required in ss. 1 and 14 TDA 1968

Liability was strict in s. 1(1)(a) inasmuch as a trader committed an offence just by innocently applying a false description to a product, as there were no defences at all. However, defences of due diligence including mistake, reliance on information provided by another, act or default of another or some other event beyond control of the trader was available under s. 24 for breaches of s. 1(1)(b), but only on proof of a lack of intent to apply a false description. Moreover, these defences were also available to a trader who falsely described a service under s. 14.

Misleading pricing under the Consumer Protection Act 1987, Part III

According to s. 20 CPA 1987, an offence was committed when a trader, in the course of a business, gave a misleading indication to a consumer of price about goods, services, accommodation or facilities. A defence of due diligence, similar to s. 24 TDA 1968, was provided by s. 39 CPA 1987.

Reform

The Consumer Protection from Unfair Trading Regulations 2008 revoked the Control of Misleading Advertisements Regulations 1988, and superseded much of the law in TDA 1968, including Part III CPA 1987. All of the previous offences under TDA 1968 and CPA 1987, Part III have been subsumed into the concept of *unfair trading practices* which include unfair actions, unfair omissions, aggressive practices, practices under a general prohibition and practices which are automatically deemed to be unfair.

■ The reforms introduced by the Consumer Protection from Unfair Trading Regulations 2008

These Regulations implemented the Unfair Commercial Practices Directive 2005/29/EC, which aims to control unfair commercial practices in business-to-consumer dealings only, unlike TDA 1968, which covers business-to-business transactions as well. Seeking **maximum harmonisation** within Member States of the EU is another aim of the Directive.

KEY DEFINITION: Maximum harmonisation

A common standard is set for all Member States of the EU to adhere to. A standard fixed to ensure complete equality of legal provision.

Key concepts in the CPUT Regulations 2008

Certain new concepts were introduced by these regulations and are defined in reg. 2(1). The most significant are: 'consumer', 'average consumer'; **trader**; 'commercial practice'; **material distortion of economic behaviour**; 'product'; **professional diligence**, and 'transactional decision'.

Consumer

A consumer is defined as a natural person who acts for purposes outside his business. The 'European' definition discards any idea of consumer status being conferred upon a business as a way of dealing.

□ REVISION NOTE

Refer to the definitions of 'consumer' given in Chapter 1.

The average and vulnerable consumer according to reg. 2(2)–(6)

An average consumer is a natural person who is defined in reg. 2(2) as being 'reasonably well-informed, reasonably observant and circumspect'. Allowance is made for targeted groups and vulnerable consumers by means of reg. 2(4) and (5) respectively.

Targeted consumer: reg. 2(4)	Vulnerable consumer: reg. 2(5)
Where the practice is directed to a particular group of consumers ... the average consumer shall ... refer to the average member of that group	(a) where a clearly identifiable group of consumers is particularly vulnerable to the practice ... because of their mental or physical infirmity, age or credulity in a way ... the trader could reasonably be expected to foresee, and (b) the practice is likely to materially distort the economic behaviour only of that group ... the average consumer shall be ... the average member of that group

 Don't be tempted to...

Don't overlook the fact that the term 'average consumer' is open to interpretation as the perception and expectations of one consumer may differ from those of another. In Chapter 1, the *Lloyd Schuhfabrik Meyer* case took into account average consumer perceptions and expectations in light of the description given to a shoe trade mark, and the context in which it was marketed. In making these kinds of assessment no consideration is given to a person's nature in the process of being a consumer.

✓ **Make your answer stand out**

The vulnerable consumer must belong to a targeted group that is clearly identified as 'vulnerable' to the product and the manner in which it is marketed. A vulnerable consumer, who happens to be a member of a group of targeted average consumers, will be judged by the reaction of those average consumers. In other words, no allowance will be made for his vulnerability. So, the vulnerable consumer will be adjudged to be 'reasonably well-informed, observant and circumspect'.

Trader

The definition given in reg. 2 seems to match the interpretation of the concept 'in the course of a business', submitted by the court in *Stevenson* v. *Rogers* (see Chapter 1).

KEY DEFINITION: Trader (under reg. 2)

This includes any natural or legal person 'acting for purposes relating to his trade, business, craft or profession'.

Make your answer stand out

It is interesting to note that the *Stevenson* v. *Rogers* interpretation of 'trader' which supports the definition in reg. 2 differs from that applied to the former Trade Descriptions Act 1968 definition in *Davis* v. *Sumner* [1984] 1 WLR 1301, which required a regular course of dealing.

Commercial practice

KEY STATUTE

Consumer Protection from Unfair Trading Regulations 2008, reg. 2(1)

A commercial practice includes:
... any act, omission, course of conduct, representation or commercial communication (including advertising and marketing) by a trader ... directly connected with promotion, sale or supply of a product to or from consumers, whether before, during or after a commercial transaction ...

Any advertising or marketing which is done *before, during or after* the transaction, counts as a commercial practice. So, a commercial practice can include advertising or marketing *after* a commercial transaction, unlike TDA 1968, where, in order to establish whether or not a false statement was an offence, there had to be a false or misleading description before or at the time of the commercial transaction.

Unfair commercial practices

Five types of commercial practice are unfair according to the following regulations:

Regulation number	A commercial practice is unfair if it:
Reg. 3(3): The General Prohibition	(a) contravenes the requirements of professional diligence; and
	(b) materially distorts (or is likely to distort) the economic behaviour of the average consumer towards the product;
Reg. 5	(c) is a misleading action;
Reg. 6	(d) is a misleading omission;
Reg. 7	(e) is aggressive; or
Sch. 1	(f) is listed on the 'black list' as always considered unfair in all circumstances

The general prohibition under reg. 3(3)

To be seen as *unfair* a commercial practice has to 'contravene the requirements of *professional* diligence'.

KEY DEFINITION: Professional diligence

The standard of special skill and care which a trader may reasonably be expected to exercise towards consumers, commensurate with either:

(a) honest market practice in the trader's field ...; or

(b) the general principle of good faith in the trader's field ...

'Honest market practice' has to be interpreted within the context of the particular trade, which may not necessarily match *ideal best practice*. For instance, a trader could diligently complete work to a mediocre standard, but not be fully competent in carrying it out.

 Make your answer stand out

The general principle of good faith is mentioned but not defined in the CPUT Regulations. Neither is it defined in the Unfair Terms in Consumer Contracts Regulations 1999, which only talks about the 'requirement of good faith' in the context of negotiation of terms between parties of unequal bargaining power. A greater conceptual understanding of what good faith refers to about a person's intentions needs satisfying, rather than it just being the outcome of the parties' trading behaviour. Whilst being unfamiliar to English law, good faith is a more utilised concept in French and German law and the ECJ may develop a 'harmonised' European concept of good faith accordingly.

A commercial practice is also seen as unfair if it *materially distorts ... the economic behaviour of the average consumer.*

KEY DEFINITION: Material distortion of average consumer's economic behaviour

To impair the average consumer's ability to make an informed decision, thereby causing him to take a transactional decision that he would not have otherwise taken (see reg. 2(1)).

Distortion of the consumer's economic behaviour is a key factor in determining whether a commercial practice is considered to be unfair. Hence, while practices like bribes, incentives and heavy persuasion may be unconscionable, they will not be seen as unfair, unless they actually *distort* the average consumer's behaviour.

! Don't be tempted to...

Be sure not to overlook the consumer's reaction to the unfair trading practice. It is the *economic behaviour* of the average consumer that must be distorted materially. Much depends on *how the consumer reacts* to the trader's unfair trading behaviour. If the consumer does not react to a trader's serious deception, then the trading practice is not seen as unfair and so no offence is committed. Because the behaviour of the consumer is the focus, were a trader to make a trivial deception, either recklessly or deliberately, and cause an average consumer to enter into a transaction, they would be liable for an unfair trading practice. The trader's state of mind in an unfair trading practice is therefore irrelevant.

KEY STATUTE

Consumer Protection from Unfair Trading Regulations, reg. 2(1)

Any decision taken by a consumer, whether it is to act or to refrain from acting concerning:

(a) whether, how and on what terms to purchase, make a payment in whole or in part for, retain or dispose of a product; or
(b) whether, how and on what terms to exercise a contractual right in relation to a product.

Taking a transactional decision under reg. 2(1)

Taking a transactional decision involves the average consumer acting in reliance upon the goodwill of the trader. Obversely, an unfair commercial practice is detrimental to a consumer in the absence of the trader's goodwill. In the TDA 1968, there was no need to show any transactional decision on the part of the customer, as a trader was liable for making a false or misleading description, *per se*.

Misleading actions under reg. 5

There are two ways in which an action can be misleading if it causes (or is likely to cause) an average consumer to take a transactional decision he would otherwise not have taken.

1. Regulation 5(2)	2. Regulation 5(3)
The commercial practice contains false information about one or more specified matters or it deceives (or is likely to deceive) an average consumer about one or more specified matters, i.e.: ■ existence or nature of product ■ main characteristics of product ■ extent of trader's commitments ■ price or manner in which price is calculated ■ need for a service, part, replacement or repair ■ nature, attributes, rights of trader(s)/agents ■ consumer rights	By means of marketing practices which either create confusion with any of the products of a competitor, or relate to breach of a code of conduct which the trader has adopted

Misleading omissions under reg. 6(1)

A commercial practice will be a misleading omission where it causes (or is likely to cause) the average consumer to make a transactional decision by making omissions as outlined below:

Examples of misleading omissions under reg. 6(1)	Factors to take into account when determining unfairness of the practice
■ Omission/hiding of *material information* ■ Provision of unclear, unintelligible, ambiguous or untimely information ■ Failure to identify commercial intent	■ All features/circumstances of the commercial practice ■ Any limitations of the medium used to communicate the commercial practice ■ If communication medium is limited, what steps were taken to use other means

Material information

Material information includes any information needed by the average consumer to make a decision to enter into a transaction, as well as any information required to be given by commercial communications as a result of a Community obligation, for example, the Electronic Commerce (EC Directive) Regulations 2002 (see Chapter 6). In the case of an invitation to purchase, the material information should include the following specific criteria:

■ The main features of the product.

■ The trader's identity.

- The geographical address of the trader.
- Either the price including taxes or the way in which the price is calculated.
- All additional freight, delivery or postal charges or a warning that they will be payable.
- The arrangements for payment, delivery, performance and complaints handling, should professional diligence not be exercised.
- The existence of rights of withdrawal or cancellation.

Regulation 6, therefore, seems to apply to all forms of material omissions of information including details about the trader's poor past or present performance.

✎ EXAM TIP

One of the aims of the Unfair Commercial Practices Directive 2005/29 is to ensure that consumers are equipped with sufficient information to make informed choices when considering a purchase. With this in mind, highlight areas within the CPUT Regulations to illustrate how any of the aims of the Directive have been implemented. This will show that you are aware of the policy underpinning the Directive and have an ability to relate this policy to the Regulations.

Aggressive commercial practices under reg. 7(1)

A commercial practice will be seen as 'aggressive' when a trader uses harassment, coercion or undue influence so that the consumer's ability to act is (or is likely to be) significantly impaired. The practice must cause the average consumer to take a transactional decision as defined in reg. 2(1) for it to be seen as unfair. Although definitions of *coercion* and *undue influence* are given in reg. 7(3), the Regulations fail to define *harassment*.

KEY STATUTE

Consumer Protection from Unfair Trading Regulations 2008, reg. 7(3)

(a) 'coercion' includes the use of physical force; and
(b) 'undue influence' means exploiting a position of power in relation to the consumer so as to apply pressure, even without using or threatening to use physical force, in a way which significantly limits the consumer's ability to make an informed decision.

Make your answer stand out

Neither of these terms is defined in the UCPD 2005, but at least they have been partially addressed in the CPUT Regulations. In the absence of a definition of 'harassment' within the Regulations a court may resort to existing statutes like the Protection from Harassment Act 1997, which provides sanctions for 'stalking' offences. It is interesting to note that this Act carries similar penalties to those in reg. 11.

Guidelines for establishing harassment, coercion or undue influence

Despite the absence of a definition for all three types of aggressive trading practices, reg. 7(2) offers guidelines on factors to be taken into account when determining when harassment, coercion or undue influence might have taken place. These factors include:

- Timing, location or persistence.
- Threatening/abusive language or behaviour.
- Exploitation by the trader of any specific misfortune, so as to impair the consumer's judgement and influence their decision.
- Onerous or disproportionate non-contractual barrier regarding the consumer's rights under the contract.
- The threat of legal action when none can legally be taken.

Commercial practices which are unfair in all circumstances under Sch. 1

Trading practices that are always unfair, whatever the circumstances, are contained as a 'black list' in Sch. 1. As there are 31 of these practices that are banned outright they are too numerous to list, but the most salient include:

- Falsely displaying a quality mark or equivalent.
- Lying about being signatory to a code of practice.
- Falsely claiming that the trader is about to cease trading.
- Falsely saying that a product has a limited time offer.
- Presenting rights given in law to a consumer as a distinctive feature of the trader's offer.
- Falsely claiming that a product is able to cure illnesses, dysfunction or malformations.
- Making persistent, unsolicited telephone calls, emails or faxes unless they are to enforce a contractual obligation.

- Asking for unnecessary documents in an insurance claim or failing to correspond on pertinent matters to discourage the consumer from pursuing their claims.

- Targeting children in advertisements to get them to buy or to persuade their parents to buy products.

- Informing the consumer that if he does not buy the product or service the trader's livelihood will be in jeopardy.

- Creating the false impression that the consumer has already won, will win, or will on doing a particular act, win a prize, when in fact there is no prize, or in claiming the prize the consumer will have to spend money or incur a cost.

- Demanding immediate or deferred payment for or the return or safekeeping of products supplied by the trader, but not solicited by the consumer (inertia selling).

KEY CASE

OFT v. *Purely Creative Ltd* [2011] EWHC 106 (Ch)

Concerning: breach of Para. 31, Sch. 1

Facts

Actually, Purely Creative Ltd was just one of many defendant marketing companies in this case. All of whom conducted what is understood to be a standard unsolicited selling ploy for enticing consumers to claim goods following their supposed entry to a fictitious prize draw. Curious consumers could only effectively claim a prize by calling a premium rate telephone number. As is usual, almost all (99.92%) of the allotted codes on letters sent to consumers matched the least expensive prize: which in the case of Purely Creative was an ersatz 'Zurich' watch.

The total cost of the watch to the defendant came to £9.36, whereas the cost incurred to most recipients was about £18.00, which included £9.50 for a six-minute premium rate telephone call, and £8.50 for postage and insurance. In fact, the defendant never bothered to insure the watch at all. There was a cheaper option to apply by post at £9.50, but to all intents and purposes this was not viable. The defendant received an income of £15.71 from each telephone applicant.

Legal principle

The defendant deliberately created a false impression of prize-winning (contrary to Para. 31, Sch. 1 to the CPUT Regulations 2008), as the consumer was required to pay for a watch by way of a procedure for claiming it. Also, it was not made clear at the outset whether the six-minute premium rate call was a *minimum* or *maximum* amount of time required to claim the prize. As it stood, all telephone calls would cost at least £8.95, anyway. Having promised that £8.50 would cover insurance as well as a fair postage charge, the defendant misled the consumer by failing to insure the watch.

Furthermore, the defendant breached reg. 5 by giving a misleading impression that the consumer had been specifically selected to win a prize, when they had not. What is more, reg. 6 was breached in that no probabilistic information was given as to the chances of winning a higher-value prize.

As Purely Creative Ltd relied on this kind of sales promotion as a means to market targeted goods, they were naturally unwilling to give the OFT an undertaking to stop these misleading practices. As a result, the OFT were granted an injunction under the Enterprise Act 2002 to ensure that the defendant ceased trading.

Unlike the other unfair trading practices covered so far, there is no requirement for the consumer to be influenced in any way whatsoever by a trader's practice. A trader will be liable automatically for carrying out the unfair trading practice, irrespective of a consumer's reaction.

Penalties for the offences

Any trader found to be carrying out any of the unfair trading practices described in the CPUT Regulations will be subject to a fine or two years' imprisonment or both, as provided by regs. 8–12.

Offence	Relevant sanction
Generally prohibited practices	reg. 8(1)(a) Any trader convicted on indictment will be subject to a fine or two years' maximum imprisonment or both.
	reg. 9: sanctions as for reg. 8 above
Misleading actions	reg. 10: sanctions as for reg. 8 above
Misleading omissions	reg. 11: sanctions as for reg. 8 above
Aggressive commercial practices	
Sch. 1 practice	reg. 12: sanctions as for reg. 8 above

Defences

Defences are given to unfair trading practices in regs. 17 and 18.

Due diligence defence under reg. 17

A trader will have a defence to all offences, except those in Sch. 1, were the commission of an offence due to:

- A mistake.
- Reliance on information provided by another.
- The act or default of another.
- An accident.
- Another cause beyond his control.

Moreover, the trader will have to show that he took all reasonable precautions and exercised due diligence to avoid the offence being committed in the first place.

✎ EXAM TIP

When discussing defences in your assessment, you should point out that reg. 17 reflects the defence given in s. 24(1) TDA 1968. Case law that was decided under this Act should be used to illustrate the operation of the defence of 'due diligence'. Indicate how the defence under s. 24(1) was used by defendants charged under s. 14 TDA 1968 in relation to falsely described services, and by those charged under s. 1(1)(b) for supplying goods with a false description. Also, point out that the defence does not apply to any offences listed under Sch. 1 to the Regulations.

KEY CASE

Tesco v. *Nattrass* [1972] AC 153
Concerning: the defence of default of another

Facts

A supermarket was running an offer on special packs of washing powder at a discounted price and displayed an advertisement to this effect within the store. When they sold out, an employee re-stacked the shelves with ordinary packs of the same brand, but his manager failed to remove the advertisement. A customer having been charged the full price for the powder, complained to the public authorities, whereon, the supermarket was duly charged with s. 1(1)(b) TDA 1968.

Legal principle

As the offence had been committed by the manager, the House of Lords accepted the defence of 'default of another', under s. 24. The store could not have been at fault, since they had taken all reasonable steps in establishing effective pricing checks.

Innocent publication of an advertisement defence under reg.18

This is the same as the s. 25 defence in the TDA 1968, and s. 24 of the CPA 1987 that concerns advertising and prices. A defence will be open to a trader, as long as he can prove that he is in the business of publishing advertisements in the ordinary course of business. Furthermore, a trader would also have to prove that they published the advertisement unaware that it would infringe the CPUT Regulations.

Enforcement powers under Part 4 of the Regulations

Criminalisation of trading activity was not a requirement of the Unfair Commercial Practices Directive 2005/29/EC; rather the UK chose to create offences as sanctions for 'rogue traders'. The primary enforcement tool is enforcement orders under the Enterprise Act 2002, s. 214 in respect of Community infringements. A duty of enforcement is given to the Office of Fair Trading and all local weights and measures authorities. Under Part 4 of the CPUT Regulations the enforcers can make test purchases, enter premises with or without a warrant, seize goods, conduct an investigation and institute a prosecution. Any trader who is found not guilty, though, will be entitled to compensation from the OFT.

The Enterprise Act (Part 8 Domestic Infringements) Order 2003 listed a number of Acts and Community instruments that qualify as subject to 'domestic' as well as 'Community' infringements. Breaches of the Regulations are now represented as Community infringements within the ambit of the Enterprise Act 2002.

Enforcement powers under the Enterprise Act 2002, Part 8

Part 8 of the Enterprise Act 2002 enables general or designated enforcers to apply for enforcement orders to prohibit infringements of domestic or Community legislation that harm the collective interests of consumers. '**Consumer**' is defined in terms of the nature of the **transaction** between the parties.

KEY DEFINITION: Consumer transaction (under the Enterprise Act 2002, s. 210)

(1) Where goods or services are ... supplied to the individual (whether by sale or otherwise) in the course of a business, and
(2) the individual receives ... the goods or services otherwise than in the course of a business.

A list of qualifying Directives and their matching domestic legislation is set out in the Enterprise Act (Part 8 Community Infringements Specified UK Laws) Order 2003. Some of them are listed below:

Directives	Specified UK laws
Council Directive 85/577/EEC	Consumer Protection (Cancellation of Contracts Concluded away from Business Premises) Regulations 1987
Council Directive 87/102/EEC	Consumer Credit Act 1974 and secondary legislation made thereunder
Council Directive 93/13/EEC	Unfair Terms in Consumer Contracts Regulations 1999
Directive 97/7/EC	Consumer Protection (Distance Selling) Regulations 2000
Directive 99/44/EC	Numerous sections in: Supply of Goods (Implied Terms) Act 1973; Sale of Goods Act 1979; Supply of Goods and Services Act 1982; Sale and Supply of Goods to Consumers Regulations 2002; Unfair Contract Terms Act 1977; and the Consumer Transactions (Restrictions on Statements) Order 1976
Directive 2000/31/EC	Electronic Commerce (EC Directive) Regulations 2002

Before applying for an enforcement order, the OFT must consult with a trader who is guilty of an infringement, except in cases where they consider enforcement must be made immediately. The main purpose of the consultation is to elicit an undertaking from the trader that they will desist from their deceptive behaviour, otherwise the OFT will use its power to apply for an enforcement order.

■ Business Protection from Misleading Marketing Regulations 2008

Businesses lost their protection when the Control of Misleading Advertising Regulations 1988 and most of the Trade Descriptions Act 1968 were repealed. Due to the lack of protection against misleading and comparative advertising, further regulations had to be introduced in the Business Protection from Misleading Marketing Regulations 2008.

Summary of the provisions of the Business Protection from Misleading Marketing Regulations 2008

Content	Explanation
Part 1: Prohibition of misleading advertising	Prohibits misleading advertising and gives the conditions under which comparative advertising is allowed. Requires that Code Owners (responsible for Codes of Practice) should not promote misleading advertising or comparative advertising that is banned.
Part 2: Criminal offences and defences	Fine or up to two years' imprisonment if convicted on indictment. Defences of due diligence and innocent publication are provided.
Part 3: Enforcement duties	The enforcement authorities include: the OFT, local weights and measures authorities and the Northern Irish Department of Enterprise, Trade and Investment. These enforcers are empowered to apply for an injunction to secure compliance with the Regulations.
Part 4: Additional powers for enforcement authorities	Include investigations into possible breaches of the Regulations, test purchases and entry into premises with or without a warrant.

■ Putting it all together

Answer guidelines

See the problem question at the start of the chapter.

Approaching the question

You are asked to advise Miss Fit regarding *criminal* rather than *civil* liability, powers of enforcement and possible defences. You will need to apply the relevant provisions of the Consumer Protection from Unfair Trading Regulations 2008 to each issue in turn.

▶

Important points to include

■ Have you outlined the aim of the UCPD?

■ With regard to liability, identify Miss Fit as a trader undertaking a commercial practice.

■ Define commercial practice.

■ Explain the five potential offences listed in the Regulations.

■ Is this commercial practice unfair according to any of these offences?

■ Is the practice a misleading action, omission or listed under Sch. 1?

■ Consider whether Mr Moan is an average consumer and, if so, if he has been targeted.

■ As regards defences, explain and apply the defence of due diligence.

With regard to enforcement, outline the duties given under Part 4 of CPUT Regulations as well as the ability to apply for enforcement orders under Part 8 of the Enterprise Act 2002.

 Make your answer stand out

Explain terms like professional diligence, material distortion and average consumer, before identifying a possible offence. Apply the guidelines given by the Regulations to the scenario in deciding whether a practice can be categorised as unfair. When considering enforcement powers, explain that it was not a requirement of the UCPD 2005 that unfair trading practices be criminalised; that was the choice of the UK government. When considering defences, apply the previous case law to indicate that the new defences mirror those in previous legislation.

READ TO IMPRESS

Cartwright, P. (1996) Reckless Statements, Trade Descriptions and Law Reform, *Northern Ireland Legal Quarterly* 47 171

Griffiths, M. (2007) Unfair Commercial Practices – A New Regime, *Communications Law* 196

Twigg-Flesner, C. *et al.* (2005) An Analysis of the Application and Scope of the Unfair Commercial Practices Directive, DTI Report

www.pearsoned.co.uk/lawexpress

 Go online to access more revision support including quizzes to test your knowledge, sample questions with answer guidelines, podcasts you can download, and more!

And finally, before the exam ...

This revision guide typically reflects the approach that is needed to formulate answers in exams – so much so that the process in summarising these topics appears much the same as answering a question on them!

First, one must identify the salient legal issue in the topic/question, and then substantiate it with legal authority by use of relevant cases/statutes. Show that you understand the legal concepts laid down in case/statute law by explaining the reasoning behind the judgments. And finally, apply the interpretation presented by the case law to the facts of the question and reason your own legal argument.

Test yourself

☐ Look at the **revision checklists** at the start of each chapter. Are you happy that you can now tick them all? If not, go back to the particular chapter and work through the material again. If you are still struggling, seek help from your tutor.

☐ Attempt the **sample questions** in each chapter and check your answers against the guidelines provided.

☐ Go online to **www.pearsoned.co.uk/lawexpress** for more hands-on revision help and try out these resources:

  ☐ Try the **test your knowledge** quizzes and see if you can score full marks for each chapter.

  ☐ Attempt to answer the **sample questions** for each chapter within the time limit and check your answers against the guidelines provided.

  ☐ Listen to the **podcast** and then attempt the question it discusses.

  ☐ **'You be the marker'** and see if you can spot the strengths and weaknesses of the sample answers.

  ☐ Use the **flashcards** to test your recall of the legal principles of the key cases and statutes you've revised and the definitions of important terms.

  ▶

☐ Practise drawing diagrams or flow charts to outline key points relating to a topic such as sale of goods, credit and unfair contract terms.

☐ Make sure you know the difference between **contractual**, **tortious** and **product liability** and the respective remedies for each head of liability.

☐ Check that you understand the nature of authority given in agency relationships.

■ Linking it all up

You need to be aware that the topics covered in this book are interrelated. To take an example, sale and supply of goods is part of contract law, as is the supply of credit, and unfair terms regulation applies to tortious as well as contractual situations. Liability for false or misleading representations is regulated by civil as well as criminal legislation, and our legislation on consumer and commercial law is now emanating from the European Union.

Check where there are overlaps between subject areas. (You may want to review the 'revision note' boxes throughout this book.) Make a careful note of these as knowing how one topic may lead into another can increase your marks significantly. Here are some examples:

✓ A false or misleading statement made by a trader can involve issues of misrepresentation, s. 13 liability for sale of goods and represent an unfair trading practice under the Consumer Protection from Unfair Trading Regulations 2008.

✓ A defective product can raise questions of liability in tort, under the Consumer Protection Act 1987 and under the Sale of Goods Act 1979. Remedies will vary according to each head of liability.

✓ Much business is now carried out by distance selling and via the web, you should be aware of how the Regulations on distance selling and electronic commerce interrelate with legislation on the sale and supply of goods and services, including credit.

■ Knowing your cases

Make sure you know how to use relevant case law in your answers. Use the table opposite to focus your revision of the key cases in each topic. To review the details of these cases, refer back to the particular chapter.

Key case	How to use	Related topics
Chapter 1 – The Need for Consumer Protection		
Lloyd Schuhfabrik Meyer & Co. GmbH v. *Klijsen Handel BV* C-342/97	To explain the nature of the average consumer's perception limitations of the role of the ECJ	Consumer Protection from unfair trading; Unfair Terms in Consumer Contracts
Stevenson v. *Rogers* [1999] 2 WLR 1064	To determine when a party is acting within the course of a business	Sale of Goods implied terms; exclusion clauses and unfair contract terms
Davis v. *Sumner* [1984] 1 WLR 1301	To show how the criminal law defines a consumer	Unfair Trading Practices under the CPUT Regulations 2008. Sale of Goods Act 1979, s. 13
Chapter 2 – Contract Terms		
Attorney General of Belize v. *Belize Telecom Ltd* [2009] UKPC 11	To explain the test used to determine implied terms	Agency law: authority by conduct
Bannerman v. *White* (1861) 10 CBNS 844	To show the difference between a representation and a term	Sections 13 and 14 SGA 1979
Director General Fair Trading v. *First National Bank* [2000] All ER 759	To outline the definition of a *core term* and *fairness*	Unfair terms in consumer contracts. Credit agreements – unfair relationships
Hong Kong Fir Shipping Co. Ltd v. *Kawasaki Kisen Kaisha Ltd* [1962] 2 QB 26 (CA)	To illustrate the operation of an innominate term	Contract terms, nature of a term, remedies for breach of contract of sale and rights to repudiate
Interfoto Picture Library v. *Stiletto Visual Programs* [1988] 2 All ER 348 (CA)	To point out the significance of giving notice of onerous terms	Unfair Terms in Consumer Contracts Regulations 1999

▶

Key case	How to use	Related topics
Chapter 2 – Contract Terms *Continued*		
Office of Fair Trading v. *Abbey National plc & Others* [2009] UKSC 6	To clarify definition of a *core* term and explain the circumstances in which the *Test of Fairness* applies	Unfair contract terms in consumer contracts; unfair relationships in credit agreements
Photo Production Ltd v. *Securicor Transport Ltd* [1980] AC 827	To demonstrate when liability can be excluded for fundamental breach of contract	Supply of Goods and Services Act 1982, ss. 13 and 16
Spurling v. *Bradshaw* [1956] 1 WLR 461	To explain the court's attitude to notice of onerous clauses by way of *the Red Hand Rule*	*Contra proferentem* interpretation of contract terms. Absence of good faith in contractual relationships
Watford Electronics Ltd v. *Sanderson CFL Ltd* [2001] EWCA Civ 317	To show how the test of reasonableness operates in cases of equal bargaining power	Contractual terms in contracts for the sale and supply of goods
Chapter 3 – Sale and Supply of Goods 1: Implied Terms		
Arcos Ltd v. *E. A. Ronaasen & Sons* [1933] AC 470	To illustrate the doctrine of strict compliance with contractual description	Rights of repudiation in contract and sale of goods
Ashington Piggeries Ltd v. *Christopher Hill Ltd* [1971] 1 All ER 847	To explain the significance of partial reliance in s. 14(3) SGA 1979	Reliance on skill and judgement of seller in misrepresentation and breach. Reasonableness factors in UCTA 1977
Feldaroll Foundry plc v. *Hermes Leasing (London) Ltd* [2004] EWCA Civ 747	To show the effect of exclusion of liability under s. 14 SGA 1979 when a company deals as a consumer	Definition of consumer status (Chapter 1). Effect of s. 6 UCTA 1977 (Chapter 2)

Key case	How to use	Related topics
Chapter 3 – Sale and Supply of Goods 1: Implied Terms *Continued*		
Grant v. *Australian Knitting Mills Ltd* [1936] AC 85 (PC)	To illustrate breach of implied terms as to quality and fitness for purpose under SGA 1979	Breach of s. 13 SGA 1979. Product liability under CPA 1987
Henry Kendall & Sons v. *William Lillico & Sons Ltd* [1969] 2 AC 31	To give an example of goods that are usable within their contract description	Sections 13 and 14(2) SGA 1979
Jewson Ltd v. *Kelly* [2003] EWCA Civ 1030	To illustrate the greater protection offered by s.14(3) over s.14 (2B)(a) and the importance of reliance on the skill and judgement of the seller	Section 14(2B)(a) and (3) SGA 1979
Microbeads AG v. *Vinehurst Road Markings* [1975] 1 WLR 218	To give an example of the right to quiet possession of goods	Breach of warranty
Niblett Ltd v. *Confectioners' Materials Co Ltd* [1921] 3 KB 387	To show when an owner may not have the right to sell goods	Remedies for breach of condition. Transfer of property in the goods (Chapter 4)
Nichol v. *Godts* [1854] 10 Exch 191	To illustrate the relationship between sale by description and sample	Breach of contract, remedies
Re Moore & Co Ltd and Landauer & Co Ltd [1921] 2 KB 519	To give an example of the effects of breach of s. 13	Rights of rejection for non-consumer buyers and consumer buyers
Reardon Smith Line Ltd v. *Yngvar Hansen-Tangen* [1976] 1 WLR 989	To demonstrate limitation of the rule of strict contractual compliance with description	Operation of s. 15A SGA 1979

▶

Key case	How to use	Related topics
Chapter 3 – Sale and Supply of Goods 1: Implied Terms *Continued*		
Rogers v. *Parish (Scarborough) Ltd* [1987] QB 933	To show how s. 14(2A) and (2B) criteria are used to determine 'merchantable' (satisfactory) quality	Remedies for breach of s. 14 SGA 1979
Rowland v. *Divall* [1923] 2 KB 500	To explain when ownership will not transfer with possession	Failure of consideration. Remedies for breach of condition
Thain v. *Anniesland Trade Centre* (1997) SLT (Sh Ct) 102	To explain the role of durability as a factor to determine satisfactory quality	Section 14 SGA 1979
Chapter 4 – Sale and Supply of Goods 2: Transfer of Property and Risk		
Aluminium Industrie Vaassen BV v. *Romalpa Aluminium* [1976] 1 WLR 676	To outline how title is reserved where goods are unmixed	Sections 17, 18, 61 SGA 1979. Remedies under s. 38: seller's lien and right of re-sale.
Eastern Distributors Ltd v. *Goldring* [1957] 2 All ER 525	To provide an example of the exercise of the rule of estoppel as an exception to the *nemo dat quod non habet* rule	Section 12(1) and (2) SGA 1979
Lewis v. *Averay* [1971] 3 All ER 907	To describe a situation where a sale was carried out by a person with voidable title	Section 12(1) SGA 1979
Re Peachdart [1983] 3 All ER 204	To illustrate the effect of reservation of title clauses on mixed goods	Section 20 SGA 1979
Re Wait [1927] 1 Ch 606	To explain how ascertainment by appropriation applies to transfer of property	Sections 20A and 20B SGA 1979

Key case	How to use	Related topics
Chapter 5 – Sale and Supply of Goods 3: Performance and Remedies		
Barry v. *Heathcote Ball & Co.* [2000] 1 WLR 1962	To give an example of damages claimed by the buyer at the available market price	Expectation loss
Charles Rickards v. *Oppenheim* [1950] 1 All ER 420	To demonstrate rights of repudiation on giving reasonable notice	Remedies for breach of condition
Clegg v. *Anderson* [2003] 2 Lloyd's Rep 32 (CA)	To explain non-acceptance of goods under s. 35(1)(a), (b) and (4)	Section 14(2A), (2B)(d) SGA 1979
Hadley v. *Baxendale* (1834) 9 Ex Ch 341	To emphasise that the rules on remoteness of damage do not apply to seller's action for the price	Remoteness of damage does apply to buyer's claim for damages under s. 53
J & H Ritchie Ltd v. *Lloyd Ltd* [2007] 1 WLR 670	To illustrate when a buyer has the right to reject goods after a repair under s. 35(6)(a)	Rights of rescission
Maple Flock Co. v. *Universal Furniture Products (Wembley)* [1934] 1 KB 148	To show how s. 31(2) applies to severable agreements	Section 15A SGA 1979, no right of rejection of whole consignment for trivial breaches
Robert A Munro & Co. Ltd v. *Meyer* [1930] 2 KB 312	To demonstrate when a buyer can repudiate the whole contract	Rights of repudiation for breach of a condition
Truk (UK) Ltd v. *Tomakidis GmbH* [2000] 1 Lloyd's Rep 543	To explain the effect of s. 35(6)(b) SGA 1979	Buyer's rights of rejection under Sale of Goods Act 1979

▶

Key case	How to use	Related topics
Chapter 6 – Distance Selling and Electronic Commerce		
Brinkibon Ltd v. *Stahag und S GmbH* [1983] 2 AC 34	To illustrate choice of jurisdiction in electronic contracts	Formation of contract
Entores Ltd v. *Miles Far East Corp* [1955] 2 QB 327	To explain the rules of communication of acceptance by electronic means	Formation of contract
Chapter 7 – Product Liability		
Abouzaid v. *Mothercare (UK) Ltd* [2000] EWCA Civ 348	To define a design defect	Expectation entitlement Pt 1, s. 3(1) CPA 1987 Satisfactory quality s. 14(2A), (2B)(d) SGA 1979 Section 11 CPA 1987, Pt II GPS Regulations 2005, reg. 5
A v. *National Blood Authority* [2001] 3 All ER 298	To explain the difference between standard and non-standard products	Expectation entitlement Pt 1, s. 3(1) CPA 1987 Defences under s. 4(1)(e) CPA 1987
Caparo Industries v. *Dickman* [1990] 1 All ER 568	To illustrate the extent of a duty of care	Fault-based liability
Donoghue v. *Stevenson* [1932] AC 562	To reiterate the principles of fault-based liability	Sections 2, 3 and 4 CPA 1987
Ide v. *ATB Sales Ltd* [2007] EWHC 1667 (QB)	To show the role of causation in proof of a defect	Fault-based liability under the *Caparo* test

Key case	How to use	Related topics
Chapter 7 – Product Liability *Continued*		
Richardson v. *LRC Products Ltd* [2000] PIQR 114 (QB)	To give an example of a manufacturing defect	Expectation entitlement Pt 1, s. 3(1) CPA 1987 Satisfactory quality Section 14(2A), (2B)(e) SGA 1979 GPS Regulations 2005, reg. 5
Shanklin Pier v. *Detel Products Ltd* [1951] 2 KB 854	To explain the concept of collateral agreements	Breach of warranty
Worsley v. *Tambrands Ltd* [2000] PIQR 95 (QBD)	To illustrate an information defect	Warnings under sale of goods, e.g. *Wornell* v. *RHM Agriculture (East) Ltd* [1987] 1 WLR 1091
Chapter 8 – Product Safety		
R v. *Birmingham CC ex parte Ferrero* [1991] All ER 530	To demonstrate waiver of the need to consult affected parties where suspension notice is served	Enforcement powers under EA 2002, Pt 8, s. 214 Consultation
R v. *Secretary of State for Health ex parte US Tobacco Int Inc* [1992] QB 353	To emphasise the need to consult affected parties	Enforcement powers under EA 2002, Pt 8, s. 214 Consultation
Chapter 9 – Consumer Credit		
Dimond v. *Lovell* [2000] 2 All ER 897	To show the distinction between a consumer credit agreement and a consumer hire agreement	Enforcement of a regulated credit agreement

▶

Key case	How to use	Related topics
Chapter 9 – Consumer Credit *Continued*		
Emma Carey & others v. *HSBC Bank plc & others* [2009] EWHC 3417 (QB)	To demonstrate that a non-compliance with formal requirements will not make a relationship unfair	UTCCR 1999, Test of Fairness
Hare v. *Schurek* [1993] CCLR 47	To explain the meaning of 'business' in the definition of non-commercial agreements	Course of a business; Section 14 SGA 1979; Section 12 UCTA 1977. *R & B Customs Brokers* v. *United Dominions Trust* [1988] 1 All ER 847
Wilson v. *First County Trust* [2003] UKHL 40	To give an example of an unenforceable credit agreement owing to improper execution	Formalities required for distance contracts, CP(DS) Regulations 2000 regs. 7 and 8
Chapter 10 – Agency Law		
Armstrong v. *Jackson* [1917] 2 KB 822	To illustrate what constitutes an agent's conflict of interest	Breach of fiduciary duty and good faith principles
Bertram, Armstrong & Co. v. *Godfray* [1838] 1 Knapp 381	To point out an agent's duty to follow the principal's instructions	Breach of contract
Clark Boyce v. *Mouat* [1994] 1 AC 428	To indicate when conflict of interest may occur with consent of both principal and third party	Intent and consent to an agreement
First Energy (UK) Ltd v. *Hungarian International Bank Ltd* [1993] 2 Lloyd's Rep 194	To show when even where a third party is alerted to agent's lack of authority the principal may still be liable for agent's acts	Implied terms as to authority of agent

Key case	How to use	Related topics
Chapter 10 – Agency Law *Continued*		
Freeman & Lockyer v. *Buckhurst Park Properties Ltd* [1964] 2 QB 480	To illustrate how a company's denial of apparent authority can be estopped	Misrepresentation
Hely-Hutchinson v. *Brayhead Ltd* [1968] 1 QB 549	To give an example of implied actual authority by conduct	Implied terms, e.g. *AG of Belize and others* v. *Belize Telecom Ltd and another* [2009] UKPC 1
Imageview Management Ltd v. *Jack* [2009] EWCA Civ 63	To give an example of an agent making a secret profit	Misrepresentation by silence. Breach of principles of good faith
Kofi Sunkersette Obu v. *A. Strauss & Co.* [1951] AC 243	To illustrate when an express term on remuneration overrides an implied term	Express and implied terms
Lloyds Bank Ltd v. *The Chartered Bank of India, Australia and China* [1929] 1 KB 40	To explain a third party's liability where they are deemed to be put on notice as to an agent's lack of authority	Implied terms
Luxor (Eastbourne) Ltd v. *Cooper* [1941] AC 108	To explain when a court will refuse to imply a term into a contract	Implied terms
Panorama Development (Guildford) Ltd v. *Fidelis Furnishing Fashions Ltd* [1971] 2 QB 711	To give an example of usual authority arising out of apparent authority	Implied terms as to authority of agent
Said v. *Butt* [1920] 3 KB 497	To show when a principal cannot sue a third party	Intention to create legal relations
Spearmint Rhino Ventures (UK) Ltd v. *HMRC* [2007] EWHC 613 (Ch)	To distinguish between agent and principal status	Bilateral agreement between parties

▶

Key case	How to use	Related topics
Chapter 10 – Agency Law *Continued*		
Springer v. *Great Western Railway Co* [1921] 1 KB 287	To show when an agency of necessity arises	Acting in good faith
Watteau v. *Fenwick* [1893] 1 QB 346	To demonstrate the operation of usual authority	Course of dealing as a reference point to determine liability
Waugh v. *H. B. Clifford & Sons Ltd* [1982] 2 WLR 679	To explain the use of implied authority by an agent to ignore a principal's express instructions	Implied terms
Chapter 11 – Liability for Unfair Trading Practices		
OFT v. *Purely Creative Ltd* [2011] EWHC 106 (Ch)	To give an example of breach of Para. 31 Sch. 1 reg. 5 and 6 of the CPUT Regulations 2008	Breach of s. 13 SGA 1979. Misrepresentation under s. 2(1) MRA 1967
Tesco v. *Natrass* [1972] AC 153	To illustrate the use of the defence of default of another	Product Safety: Part II, s. 39 CPA 1987, GPSR 2005, reg. 29

■ Sample question

Below is a problem question that incorporates overlapping areas of the law. See if you can answer this question drawing upon your knowledge of the whole subject area. Guidelines on answering this question are included at the end of this section.

PROBLEM QUESTION

Amir, a football manager with an interest in racing horses, decided to buy a stallion, Eros, from Ned. During negotiations for the sale, Amir told Ned that he wished to race Eros for five years and then retire him for breeding purposes, whereupon Ned said: 'He's a great runner and as regards to breeding, don't worry on that score, he should live up to his name!' Amir signed the contract of sale and paid £50,000 for the horse.

Although the horse turned out to be a successful racer, he showed no interest in breeding and on examination by a vet, three months after the sale, Eros was declared to be sterile. When Amir complained to Ned, his attention was drawn to the conditions of sale which stated:

1. All our horses are sold on the understanding that the purchasers will obtain a full veterinary report at their own expense within one month of sale. No refunds will be given after one month.
2. We are not liable for any representations made by our staff during negotiations for sale about the condition of our horses.

Advise Amir, who wishes to claim £50,000 and £10,000 loss of expected profits for stud fees.

■ Answer guidelines

Approaching the question

There are several overlapping issues here including misrepresentation, breach of contract for sale of goods, ss. 13 and 14, as well as loss of right to reject. You also need to address the effect of exclusion of liability in cases where the purchaser is dealing as a business and as a consumer.

Important points to include

As regards Ned's statement:

■ Was it a representation or a term?

■ On the issue of misrepresentation, is it actionable? This will involve using case law to distinguish fact from opinion and establish reliance and inducement.

■ If Ned's statement was a term of the contract of sale, is this a sale by description under s. 13 SGA 1979? Is the horse fit for purpose under s. 14(3)(a)?

Finally, has Amir accepted the horse under s. 35(2)(a)?

How effective are the exclusion clauses against Amir as a business and as a consumer, bearing in mind clause 1 appears to be limiting Amir's right to examine the goods within a reasonable time after delivery?

Don't forget to address damages for (a) misrepresentation under both common law and MRA 1967 and (b) damages for breach of contract including remoteness of damage.

▶

Make your answer stand out

Pick out relevant facts to apply the law; for instance, emphasise Amir's possible lack of expertise to apply the skill and knowledge test to assessing the nature of Ned's statement. Apply Lord Wilberforce's dicta in *Reardon Smith Line* that a sale is a sale by description only if the description applies to a significant part of the horse's identity. Link this with fitness for purpose and apply *Henry Kendall & Sons* to highlight that the horse was unfit for only one purpose, but point out that Amir did inform Ned as to a particular purpose for use of the horse. You need to focus on the test of reasonableness when addressing the exclusion clauses and it may be advantageous to point out that if the sale is one by description and Amir was dealing as a consumer, then clause 2 will be ineffective. Don't forget to show your awareness of the different measure of damages for misrepresentation and breach and highlight the fact that the test is one of consequential loss under s. 2(1) MRA 1967, whereas with breach of contract it will involve issues of remoteness of damage.

Glossary of terms

The glossary is divided into two parts: key definitions and other useful terms. The key definitions can be found within the chapter in which they occur, as well as in the glossary below. These definitions are the essential terms that you must know and understand in order to prepare for an exam. The additional list of terms provides further definitions of useful terms and phrases which will also help you answer examination and coursework questions effectively. These terms are highlighted in the text as they occur but the definition can only be found here.

■ Key definitions

Acceptance	An unconditional acceptance of all the terms of an offer.
Adequacy of consideration	Consideration need not be of equal value to the promise in a transaction.
An agent	He who acts through another acts for himself: *qui facit per alium, facit per se.*
Ascertained goods	Goods become ascertained once they have been identified and agreed upon, after the contract of sale.
A title or a right of ownership	An owner has exclusive rights and control over their property. The property in the goods is an example of a right of ownership.
Bill of exchange	A negotiable instrument that is similar to a cheque. A person orders their bank to pay the bearer a fixed sum of money, but on a specific date.
Business liability	Liability incurred by a person acting within the course of a business.
Cancellable agreement	This is an agreement signed by a debtor away from the trade premises of the creditor or supplier, which may be cancelled as long as it was not secured on land.

Caveat emptor	Let the buyer beware.
Consideration	What each party gives to another in an agreement: usually the price for which a promise is bought.
Consumer credit agreement	An agreement between an individual (the debtor) and any other person (the creditor) by which the creditor provides the debtor with credit of any amount.
Consumer transaction	This is a transaction whereby a consumer deals with another party who is carrying out their trade or business.
'Consumer transaction' under the Enterprise Act 2002, s. 210	1. Where goods or services are ... supplied to the individual (whether by sale or otherwise) in the course of a business; and 2. the individual receives ... the goods or services otherwise than in the course of a business.
Contra proferentem	In cases where a court determines a term to be ambiguous, a contractual interpretation will be construed against the interests of the party who insisted on its inclusion in the agreement.
Core terms	These are terms that either define the subject matter of a contract, or are concerned with the adequacy of the contract price.
'Damage' under s. 5 CPA 1987	1. Death or personal injury caused by the defect 2. Damage to property (non-business use only) worth more than £275 3. Not the damaged product itself.
Disclosed principal	A principal is disclosed when he is named or when the agent indicates that he is acting on behalf of a principal.
Distance contract	One which is between a supplier acting for commercial or professional purposes and a *consumer* who is a natural person acting for purposes outside his business. It must concern goods or services and be conducted under an *organised distance sales or service scheme* run by the supplier. Finally, the supplier must make exclusive use of distance communications such as telephone, fax, television, letter, email, internet, up to and at the time the contract is made.
Distributor under reg. 2 GPS Regs 2005	One who knowingly supplies a product that is patently unsafe.

Exclusion or exemption clause	A term or notice that attempts to exclude or restrict liability for one's acts or omissions.
Expectation loss	Damages that aim to fulfil a contract by placing a party in the position they would have been in were the contract carried out, which may include loss of expected profits.
Express terms	Terms that are written or spoken.
Force majeure clause	A clause which allocates risk in the event of something that might happen.
Harmonise	To make laws the same or similar.
Hire purchase	A person, otherwise known as a *bailee*, agrees to hire goods on credit terms for a fixed period of time, with an option to buy (for a nominal fee) at the end of the agreed period.
Implied terms	Terms that are not written or spoken, but implied in a variety of ways.
Legal intent	Where both parties intend the agreement to have legal effect.
Lien	The right to hold onto the property of another and keep it as security until an obligation has been performed.
'Material distortion of average consumer's economic behaviour' under CPUTR 2008	To impair the average consumer's ability to make an informed decision, thereby causing him to take a transactional decision that he would not have otherwise taken (reg. 2(1)).
Maximum harmonisation	A common standard to adhere to is set for all Member States of the EU. A standard fixed to ensure complete equality of legal provision.
Misrepresentation	A false statement of *fact* made to *induce* a party into a contract.
Nemo dat quod non habet	No one can sell what he does not have.
Non-commercial agreement	A consumer credit or hire agreement not made by a creditor or owner in the course of a business carried out by him.
Personal remedies	Remedies sought personally against the buyer for compensation of loss.
'Professional diligence' under CPUTR 2008	The standard of special skill and care which a trader may reasonably be expected to exercise towards consumers, commensurate with either:
	'… honest market practice in the trader's field … or the general principle of good faith in the trader's field …'.

Real remedies	Remedies sought against the goods themselves, in order that they may be retained by the seller.
Reliance loss	Damages to put a party back into a pre-contractual position in order to compensate for out-of-pocket losses.
Repudiate	A person shows by words or conduct that they do not see themselves as being bound by a contractual obligation. An example is where a person refuses to perform according to the terms of a contract.
Rescission	Sets the contract aside and restores parties to pre-contractual position.
Safe	Dangers posed by the goods themselves rather than their quality (CPA 1987, Pt II, s. 19).
'Service provider' under the Electronic Commerce Regulations 2002	A broad definition is given by reg. 2(1) to include: '… any service normally provided for remuneration at a distance by means of electronic equipment for the processing (including digital compression) and storage of data, and at the individual request of a recipient of a service'.
Severable contract	This term refers to a contract that can be divided individually with each part being treated separately.
Unascertained goods	Any goods that have not been identified and agreed upon at the time of the contract are considered to be unascertained, including those chosen from an identified bulk.
Undisclosed principal	A principal is undisclosed when the agent does not reveal that he is acting on behalf of a principal.
Unsolicited goods	Unrequested goods sent to the *offeree* without their consent.
Void	Has no legal effect.

▌Other useful terms

Bailee	A person who takes possession of goods with the owner's (bailor's) consent.
Condition	A term that goes to the root of a contract, the breach of which allows the other party to end the contract.
Fiduciary	A person who, in a position of trust, acts on behalf of another.

∍mnify	To make good a loss which a person has suffered because of the act or default of another.
ɪnertia selling	This is when a business tries to sell a product to a consumer by sending them unsolicited goods.
Mitigate	A duty to act reasonably, for example to reduce one's losses in a contractual claim.
Offer	An expression of willingness to be legally bound.
Penalty clause	This is a clause that is not a genuine pre-estimation of loss, but more of a 'frightener' (*in terrorem*) to be used to compel performance of a contract.
Privity of contract	A rule whereby only the parties to a contract can enforce rights or obligations under that contract.
'Producer' under s. 1(2) CPA 1987	A producer of the product; an own-brander; a business importer of goods from outside the EU; anyone subjecting agricultural produce to an industrial process.
'Product' under s. 1(2) CPA 1987	'… any goods or electricity [including] a product which is comprised in another product as a component or raw material'.
Quantum meruit	A claim for payment to reflect what a person deserves.
Regulated agreement	A consumer credit or hire agreement which is not exempt under the Consumer Credit Act 1974.
Rescind	Relieve the parties of any further obligation to perform the contract.
Reservation of title clause	A clause whereby the seller of goods can reserve property rights over the goods.
Restricted-use credit	Credit is supplied by the creditor to a supplier for a specific use.
Romalpa clause	Retention of title clauses: provide the seller with the power to retain ownership of goods until they have been paid for by the buyer.
Running-account credit	Credit is supplied indefinitely up to a limited amount and can be used by the debtor for several contracts as long as the debtor makes regular (monthly) repayments.
Uberrimae fidei	'Of the utmost good faith.' This demand is usually made in contracts such as those of insurance where all known facts must be disclosed to the insurer before the contract is entered into.

Unrestricted-use credit	Credit is given by the creditor direct to the debtor for either specific or non-specific use.
Voidable	Where a contract is capable of being set aside by one party. Until that party elects to set it aside, the contract has full legal effect.
Warranty	In a contract this is a term which, if breached, gives rise to a claim in damages rather than the right to end the contract.